The Creative Spirit

Dr June Boyce-Tillman is a composer with particular interests in the musical development of children, music and theology and women and church music. Her works have been performed in Westminster Abbey and in numerous cathedrals in the UK, as well as overseas, and have been published in a variety of books including *Reflecting Praise* (Stainer and Bell), *The Oxford Assembly Book* (OUP) and *Light the Candles* (CUP).

She founded the Hildegard Network, an international organisation concerned with bringing together the areas of theology, the arts and healing. She is a popular workshop leader and is presently Reader in Community and Performing Arts at King Alfred's College, Winchester.

Other titles in the *Rhythm of Life* series

RHYTHM of LIFE

SERIES EDITOR: BISHOP GRAHAM CHADWICK

THE CREATIVE SPIRIT

*Harmonious Living with
Hildegard of Bingen*

June Boyce-Tillman

CANTERBURY
PRESS
Norwich

First published in 2000 by The Canterbury Press Norwich
(a publishing imprint of Hymns Ancient & Modern Limited,
a registered charity)
St Mary's Works, St Mary's Plain
Norwich, Norfolk, NR3 3BH

British Library Cataloguing in Publication Data

A catalogue record for this book is available
from the British Library

ISBN 1-85311-365-4

Typeset by Rowland Phototypesetting Ltd,
Bury St Edmunds, Suffolk
Printed in Great Britain by
Biddles Ltd, Guildford and King's Lynn

Contents

ACKNOWLEDGEMENTS

I am very grateful to a number of people who have offered me advice and encouragement in this project. My colleagues in the Hildegard Network have played a significant part in my own exploration into Hildegard's life and work. The Hessische Landesbibliothek gave me access to the Riesenkodex. Myra Poole has been a real companion on the way sharing her own insights in her work on Julie Billiart. Michael Finnissy has encouraged my own musical exploration along with Michael Fields and Ansy Boothroyd. My readership at King Alfred's Winchester has enabled me to compose and perform many works including the two operas which encapsulate much of my thinking. The theologians Grace Jantzen, Mary Grey, Nancy Fierro and Elizabeth Stuart have influenced the theological reflection considerably. The academics who have written the texts listed in the bibliography have been companions along the way, sometimes in live meetings and sometimes simply through their words on the page. I am grateful to Jean Moore for permission to use her beautiful version of Hildegard's story. My son Matthew and his wife Andrea have offered much support, and my son Richard has offered much practical advice and support in terms of word processing. Finally I am grateful to Bishop Graham and the Canterbury Press for encouraging me to embark on this project and to Christine Smith for her patience and understanding in editing the text.

The book is dedicated to three of my spiritual directors: Ian Ainsworth Smith, Penelope Eckersley and Andrew Todd.

Series Introduction

'Wisdom is to discern the true rhythm of things:
joy is to move, to dance to that rhythm.'

This series of books on various traditions of Christian spirituality is intended as an introduction for beginners on the journey of faith. It might help us discover a truer rhythm as something of the experience of those who follow any particular tradition resonates with our own.

Too much can be made of the distinctions between the different expressions of Christian spirituality. They all derive from the experience of what God has done and is doing in us and among us. While emphases differ, their validity is their congruence with the good news of Jesus Christ in the scriptures. As the various instruments in an orchestra make their special contribution to the symphony, so we delight in the extra dimension that each tradition brings to the living out of the Christian faith.

The present wide interest in spirituality seems to indicate that, in the midst of all the current uncertainties that we meet in contemporary life, despite its relative comfort and technological advance, there is felt a need to reconnect with our spiritual roots and find a deeper purpose for living.

Each volume offers an introduction to the essential

elements of the particular spiritual tradition and practical guidance for shaping our everyday lives according to its teaching and wisdom. It is an exploration into the way that spiritual practice can affect our lifestyle, work, relationships, our view of creation, patterns of prayer and worship, and responsibilities in the wider world.

Many books, of course, have been written in all of these areas and in each tradition classic commentaries are available which can never be surpassed. The aim of this series is to meet the needs of those searching for or beginning to explore the journey inward into their inmost being and outward to relationship with people and the whole of creation.

This addition to the seies provides a comprehensive account of the life and work of Hildegard, visionary, composer of music, homeopathic healer, powerful preacher, counsellor to kings and popes, author of theological and other writings and the founder of an abbey at Bingen in Germany.

This remarkable woman of the twelfth century has a special message for us today when we are becoming more aware of the importance and urgency of ecology, justice and connectedness. We owe a great debt of gratitude to Dr June Boyce-Tillman for making Hildegard come alive for us. The exercises at the end of each chapter encourage us to engage with heart as well as head inwhat she has to give us.

Bishop Graham Chadwick
Salisbury
August 2000

PREFACE

Hildegard of Bingen (1098–1179) was a visionary, a musician, a poet, a theologian, a dramatist, and an abbess. She lived in an age which had not yet broken up knowledge in the fragmented way that we experience today. As such she provides us with a way '*to look again at a divided world and see it whole*', as Schumacher puts it. She gained considerable standing in her own day, illustrated by such phenomena as the number of eminent people who consulted her (including Bernard of Clairvaux and the Emperor Barbarossa), her travels and the fact that her music was written down. Nicknamed the Sybil of the Rhine, she founded two communities at Bingen and Eibingen, but established no school of spirituality or theology. She manifested a (perhaps terrifying) creativity which she saw as coming directly from God. This was expressed in a variety of ways – through the arts, theology, science, healing and justice-seeking. Remembered in Germany largely for her holistic approach to healing, she fell into obscurity until the work of Matthew Fox in the area of creation spirituality rediscovered her work.

This book will examine various aspects of her life and work. Chapters 1 and 2 will place her in her historical context. Chapter 3 will look at the notion of justice which infuses all her thinking. She is concerned for the unity of all creation: human beings, the divine and the natural world are seen to be in intimate relationship and blossom and flourish when they are in right relationship. Flowing from this, she has a deep passion and yearning for justice. For her sin was ecological – a cosmic split – not a personal issue but a political one. This finds its expression in the spiritual exercises that appear at the end of each chapter. Each of these has a meditative aspect but also suggestions as to how this might be translated into action.

Chapter 4 places her work in the context of the prayer life of her monastic community and shows how the expression of her insights involved collaborative work. Chapter 5 examines how her search for an authoritative voice grew out of her study of the Wisdom literature of the Old Testament. Out of this she generated a number of divine female figures notably the Virtues, Synagogue and Ecclesia – the Church. Here in her theology of Wisdom and the Virgin Mary she explores the feminine in God. Her attitude to the feminine is not entirely straightforward and some of her views are unfashionable today. Nevertheless, she was a strong and passionate woman on a real search for her own integrity within God.

Chapter 6 looks at her visionary experience in which her theology originated as an intuitive way of knowing. Chapter 7 looks at her medical works and approach to healing as the restoration of balance set in the context of the humourial system of medicine dominant at that time. Chapter 8 looks at her music, the way it was received and its central role in her theology.

Chapter 9 looks at Hildegard's contemporary relevance, and how the dominant values of our culture have subjugated various ways of knowing that are found in Hildegard's work. These concern connectedness, community, passionate and committed knowing, holistic approaches to healing, the valuing of process and creativity in context.

Chapter 10 turns to the concept of *viriditas* – greening power – which flows through the whole creation bringing fruitfulness. It is our responsibility to express this creatively and suggestions are made for this in terms of prayerful activity. The idea of creativity being a form of re-integration is suggested and you are encouraged to continue your own creative journey.

The book charts the process of knowing as linked with the flowing of energy through the cosmos. Hildegard's sense of the original goodness of all things led her to a faith not based on guilt but on trust, lifting her hands to God that she might be carried as a feather, without power or strength of its own, is carried on the breath of the wind.

In this book I have used her as a guide for our own journeys. I have taken themes from her writing, contemporising them in the spiritual exercises. Each chapter starts with one of her antiphons and then proceeds by means of many quotations from her work.

It has been difficult to make a selection from a woman with so many strands in her work and I hope that some may be inspired to go further into her thinking. In the bibliography further reading is suggested and also recordings of her music that may be used as an accompaniment to prayer.

Above all, Hildegard offers us an authoritative call to

embark on our own explorations into God. I trust that you will find her a helpful companion on your own spiritual journey.

June Boyce-Tillman
December 1999

Note on inclusive language

Some of the translations used in this book do not use inclusive language for human beings (or God). I decided that to insert the customary [sic] intruded on the texts too much. However, I wish to make it clear that this is not in keeping with the author's preferred position on inclusive language.

A Chronology of Hildegard's life

1098–1105 Childhood

- Born in Bermersheim, tenth and last child of Hildebert and Mechtild
- Experiences visions

1106–1136 The Oblate

- Enters the enclosure with Jutta of Sponheim, attached to the newly founded Benedictine monastery at Disibodenberg
- Takes her vows and receives the veil from Bishop Otto of Bamberg
- Tells Jutta about her visions

1136–1141 The Magistra

- Jutta dies
- Is elected Magistra
- Abbot Kuno and the Archbishop of Mainz are informed of her visions

1141–1148 The Visionary

- Receives a confirming vision and experiences a spiritual awakening
- Starts to write *Scivias* with the help of Volmar and Richardis of Stade
- Exchanges letters with Bernard of Clairvaux asking for support
- Receives affirmation from Pope Eugenius III
- Enters into a correspondence with people from many walks of life
- A letter from Master Odo of Paris indicates that her songs are becoming more widely known

1148–1159 The Abbess

- Falls seriously ill
- Inspired to move to the Rupertsberg in Bingen which she achieves after struggles with the monks of the Disibodenberg
- Writes her medical and scientific works
- Completes *Scivias*
- Begins to supervise the painting of her visions
- Begins *The Book of Life's Merits*
- Her close friend, Richardis, leaves to become abbess of a north German convent and subsequently dies
- Achieves financial independence from Disibodenberg for her community of between eighteen and twenty nuns

1159–1167 The Preacher

- Undertakes first preaching tour along the River Main to Bamberg
- Completes *The Book of Life's Merits*
- Victor IV the first anti-pope appointed
- Undertakes the second and third preaching tours including Trier and Cologne
- Sermons are disseminated
- Starts *The Book of Divine Works*

1167–1179 The Holy Woman

- Founds the second community at Eibingen which she visits twice a week
- Writes to Henry II of England and his wife, Queen Eleanor
- Falls ill again
- Heals the possessed woman, Sigewize
- Writes *The Life of St Disibod* and *The Life of St Rupert*
- Fourth preaching tour
- Volmar, her secretary, dies
- Completes *The Book of Divine Works*
- There are disputes about Volmar's successor
- Godfrey begins to write to *The Life of Hildegard*
- Guibert of Gembloux appointed as her secretary
- Prelates of Mainz impose interdict on her convent forbidding her to receive communion or sing the Office
- The interdict is lifted

- Hildegard dies
- Theodoric completes Books Two and Three of *The Life of Hildegard*
- She is accepted as a local saint
- Attempts at canonisation fail

HILDEGARD'S STORY

I am Hildegard
I know the cost of keeping silent.
And I know the cost of speaking out
Hear my story.

Perhaps you know me as Hildegard of Bingen. It was several miles from Bingen that I was born, in the Nahe Valley in Germany, in the year of Our Lord 1098. Do you know the Rhineland? It is the most beautiful place – rich and green, moist and fruitful. The rolling hills stretch as far as the eye can see, crowned with lush forests pierced here and there with rocky crags and tall watchtowers. Below, the deep valleys are dotted with neat villages and tidy fields that yield ample sustenance for all humankind and their beasts. On the southern slopes, the carefully tended vineyards ripple like green waves lapping the skirts of the hills. And through it all flows the mighty river Rhine bringing life and greenness to the land, moisture to the air, and the means of movement and transport to all who live there. They call it now, I believe, the Fatherland, but to me it will always be Mother.

For the earth is our mother, she is mother of all that is natural, all that is human. She is the mother of us all, for she contains within herself the seeds of all.

The earth of humankind contains all moistness, all verdancy, all germinating power. It is fruitful in so many ways. All creation comes from it. Yet it contains not only the basic raw material of humankind, but also the substance of the incarnation of God's son.

Being the tenth child, I was tithed to God, and sent at the age of eight to live with Jutta, a holy anchoress, who lived in a small house attached to the abbey of St Disibod. From Jutta I learned so much: of everyday things, of the ever-present, all-encircling love of God (we are embraced by him), and of the Holy Spirit which flows like sap through our souls, bringing growth and fruitfulness. From my earliest childhood God revealed himself to me in many vivid ways: sometimes in words, sometimes images, sometimes music, sometimes all three, but always he showed himself in the splendour of the natural world. And I learned to see also the evil in the world – the injustice, the corruption of state and church, and sloth and carelessness of priests, the violation of the natural world and the denial of the giftedness of all creation. And I knew anger as well as joy. I looked and listened, I saw and I heard, but I kept silent.

Yet ever within me grew the pressure to speak out. But how could I, a woman, make my voice heard? Who would listen to me? Who would believe my words, not learned by rote from any human tutor? How could my words in any way be useful? I consulted my superiors and my spiritual director – people I was accustomed to respect and obey. They told me firmly it was not my place to speak out, my role was to tend the daily needs of my community and to pray ever faithfully – but silently. Eventually I became ill both physically and mentally. How could I then have recognised within me the burning torment spoken of by the prophets of the Old Testament, when the Word of God burns in the heart and aches in the bones? It was not out of stubbornness, but out of supposed humility that I refused to speak, and I felt myself pressed down by the whip of God into a bed of sickness.

But behold in the forty-third year of my life's course, I was taken up in a vision. In great fear and trembling I beheld a great radiance, and in it was formed a voice and the voice spoke to me, saying: 'O frail human being, ash of ash, corruption of corruption, tell and write what you see and hear.' And so I rose up and set my hand to writing and behold, great power and strength were given me and I no longer felt beaten down. The words poured out of me in a torrent, a great overflowing of God's World, his Spirit . . . And contrary to all my previous fears and timidity, I was heard, I began to set down my many visions in my first book which I called *Scivias* – Knowing the Way. It was to take me ten years to complete. People came to me from far and wide asking for spiritual advice and I entered into correspondence with many of the great folk of my day – rulers, nobles, leaders of religious communities – among them the Emperor Barbarossa and Bernard of Clairvaux. The Holy Father heard of me and when he came to a Papal Council in Trier, sent a commission to investigate me. They found me competent and authentic, and he wrote, commending and encouraging my writing.

By this time Jutta had died and I had been elected

leader – abbess, you might say – of our small community of women. We had grown in numbers and more were coming every year, yet we were still crammed into Jutta's tiny house. The monastery of St Disibod had expanded too, taking up all the available land for their farms and buildings and they would not yield us an extra inch of space. At first I became anxious, then angry. Abbot Kuno was implacable. Can you imagine the endless committee meetings, the pleadings, the arguments, the counter-arguments and the endless frustration of not being heard? Eventually, we just packed our things and left, taking our dowries with us, without waiting for the men's permission.

After much hardship we began to build a new house near Bingen which I dedicated to my dear St Rupert. I myself supervised the building, making sure that all was spacious and comfortable. We even had piped water. Perhaps I remembered all those cold winter mornings, the journeys to the well and the breaking of ice on the washing trough. But more, I was concerned because I do not think our Creator God delights in our bodily discomfort, especially when it is self-inflicted. It has been said that the body is at war with the soul, but how can this be? He made us as whole beings and our souls can only find expression through the actions of our bodies. For I am persuaded that when the body and the soul act together in proper agreement, they receive the highest award of mutual joy.

In the years that followed, my sisters and I at St Rupertsberg found new ways to worship God – in poetry, music and drama, sometimes wearing colourful robes and golden crowns – not, I may say, always with

ecclesiastical approval! I continued to write and to set
down in words and pictures the many visions in which
God had become known to me. I wrote many books on
a variety of subjects, including medicine and natural
history as well as theology and the lives of the saints.
My vast correspondence continued. When in my sixties
I began to travel the length and breadth of Germany
and I, a woman, preached from the pulpits of the great
cathedrals and abbeys. Whenever I spoke of God's justice I exhorted the leaders of the church and state to
excise corruption and to work for the peace and harmony of all creation.

And in it, through it and round it was always the
music, for music expresses most deeply the soul's yearning to sing praises to its Creator, and echoes most clearly
the harmony of heaven.

But in the last year of my life the music was silenced.
It was a time of great grief and heavy sadness. We had
buried in our cemetery a young man who had been
excommunicated as a revolutionary and we refused to
yield up his body. He had confessed and received absolu-
tion before he died and his bones were entitled to rest
in hallowed ground. We were placed under an interdict
by the Archbishop and forbidden to sing the office or
to receive communion. I myself, though old and ill, went
to the cemetery and removed all traces of the grave that
it might not be violated, for I fear the justice of God
more than the justice of men. Instructed in a vision, I
wrote to the Archbishop, asking him to lift the interdict
and reminding him that those who silence music in this
life can have no fellowship with the praise of the angels
in heaven. The interdict was lifted and the music con-

tinued but the words and songs I uttered came from no human voice; they were given to me in visions. God moves where he wills, and not to the glory of any earthly creature. But I am ever in fear and trembling, doubting my own capacities. But I lift my hands to God, that he may carry me as a feather, without power or strength of its own, is carried on the breath of the wind.

I died in the year 1179, but death did not silence me. Some of you, today, may hear my voice. I was eighty-one years old and so had kept silent for half my life and had spoken for half my life. Perhaps that is the right balance: taking in, receiving, and giving out. In and out – like breathing – like the breath of God.

Jean Moore

2

A WOMAN OF HER TIME

Antiphon: To Virgins and Innocents

O most noble, greening, creative force,
Who are rooted in sunlight,
And who in their radiant
Serenity shine like a wheel of lights;
No earthly power can ever fully comprehend
Such excellence.
You are closely held in warm embrace by the Mystery
   of the Divine One.
You blush like the dawn twilight,
And burn like the flaming sunshine.[1]

In the eleventh century, Europe was beginning to recover after a period of instability. Agriculture was yielding more and there was a new sense of purpose. There was urban growth and the development of new religious orders such as the Cistercians and Carthusians. Local rulers had increasing power and were frequently in dispute with the bishops who often had temporal as well as spiritual power, complicated by the fact that the bishops were in many cases drawn from the ranks of the aristocracy. It was a time of fluctuating fortunes for leaders in both church and state. All this gave impetus to an urge for expansion resulting in the First Crusade in 1099.

In the midst of this, Hildegard shines among the

virgins identified in the antiphon above. Many claims have been made for Hildegard in contemporary writing and it is, of course, impossible to see her with spectacles completely cleansed of the intervening eight hundred or so years. But this chapter is an attempt to do just that by linking the stages of her life, described in Chapter 1, with the surrounding culture which was composed of a complex interweaving of politics, the aristocracy, monasticism and the church hierarchy.

Hildegard represents an astonishing blend of the radical and the conservative. She was the first woman to write books with the approval of the Pope and the only woman whose authority was accepted in the area of Christian doctrine. She was one of the first women composers in Europe to have their music written down and the only one to leave a large body of musical works. Her morality play with music is the first known example of its kind, prefiguring the later development of the operatic form, and the only twelfth-century piece by a named playwright. She was the first scientific writer to write on women's sexuality and childbirth. She was the only known medieval woman to have ecclesiastical approval for preaching to clergy and laity.

And yet in some ways Hildegard was extremely orthodox. Her interpretations of her remarkable visions reveal that she believed, for example, that the unbaptised receive eternal torment, and in one she saw deformed children as a reproof for the sins of their parents. These interpretations have a strongly didactic feel about them and are often in tune with her own aspirations. She managed with some difficulty to keep a balance between the prophetic and the political in her life. Without her political acumen she would not have received the support of the church authorities. She produced radical ideas in the context of an orthodox theology. It is possible also that the lack of clarity in some of her writing might be a deliberate ploy to enable her to appear orthodox to the authorities but more radical to her own community. Her ideas at times show a remarkable mixture of contempt and respect for the patriarchal structures that would have shaped her early life, both as a member of the aristocracy and as a child oblate. The unsolicited letters she wrote to leaders of church and state draw on God's authority for her calls for justice. But it is clear that she genuinely believed her own principles to be those of God and this enabled her to approach higher authorities with confidence.

Hildegard's attitude to the position of women contains a number of inconsistencies. She thought that women should know their place in society because of their infirmity and weakness and in order to fulfil their role of childbearing and believed that they should not be ordained as priests. Gender and class interact in the struggles that she entered into concerning their role. It was undoubtedly easier for her as an aristocratic woman to resolve her dilemmas about male and female authority. She often refers to the age in which she lived as 'womanish', indicating that the men had become weak, sensual and generally lax in their observance of moral codes. The reason that God had raised up a 'virile' woman was because the male ecclesiastical authorities had failed to fulfil their vocation. This represented an important development in Western mysticism: the visionary experience could now be seen as a valid route to divine truth alongside the better-established routes of prayerful study and scholarly discourse. This development enabled women visionaries of later times to claim spiritual authority and a part in the development of Western mysticism.

The Sources

Hildegard's three main theological works are *Scivias (Knowing the Way)*, *The Book of Life's Merits (Liber Vitae Meritorum)* and *The Book of Divine Works (Liber Divinorum Opera)*. The writing of these spans almost her entire adult life and they show her developing theology from her visionary experiences. Her medical and scientific books were written alongside the theological works and are regarded by some scholars as not having the same authoritative status. *The Life of St Hildegard (Vitae Hildegardis)* was written as a hagiography towards the end of her life, possibly with the intention of securing her canonisation. To achieve this it ascribes as much as possible to the hand of God; so her miracles and prophetic role are emphasised. The *Life* concentrates on the period from her call in 1141 to the establishment of the new house in 1155 and has little to say of her earlier life or her later years. It was started by the monk, Godfrey around 1174–5. Unfortunately he died before Hildegard and the work was taken over after her death by Theodoric, a staunch admirer, who had not known her personally and was chosen for his literary prowess. He used pieces dictated by Hildegard herself which he interspersed with his own adulation. The final text has three elements: Hildegard's own accounts, the work of Godfrey who worked for her, and of Theodoric who admired her from afar.

Hildegard's work was validated in her lifetime by her teacher, the Abbot of Disibodenberg, the Archbishop of Mainz, the synod of bishops at Trier, Bernard of Clairvaux and Pope Eugene III. The papal affirmation enabled her to complete her work on *Scivias* and publish it and then to break away from the monastery of St Disibod and found her house at the Rupertsberg in Bingen.

She was an avid letter writer and it is from the letters that we gain the clearest picture of her relations and the surrounding culture.

Childhood – Hildegard's Relations with the Aristocracy

Hildegard was born into a noble Rhineland family to members of the free nobility called Hildebert and Mechtild in 1098. She was the youngest in a family of ten and received visions from the age of three. She found it difficult to share these with anyone and was frequently ill as a result of them. Her parents were probably relieved to have their unusual sickly child oblated to the monastery.

We know little of her early life but her view of the world was shaped significantly by her aristocratic background. Following the common practice of her day, she recruited largely aristocratic women to her convent. For this she was criticised by the abbess Tenxwind of Andernach who reminded her that Jesus recruited humble fishermen. She replied with her usual vigour saying that although God loved all classes, different classes could not be expected to live together, likening this to herding cattle, sheep and goats into a single barn. In later life her connections with the aristocracy were to get her out of a number of difficult situations. For example, when she wanted to leave Disibodenberg, she was able to secure support for her scheme from the Marchioness of Stade.

Oblature – Hildegard's Education

At eight Hildegard left her aristocratic home to live under the tutelage of Jutta of Sponheim, an anchoress attached to the Abbey of St Disibod. With her she was able to share her visionary experiences. At around fifteen she took her religious vows and received her veil from Bishop Otto of Bamberg.

Throughout her life Hildegard claimed to be '*indocta*' (usually translated as uneducated). And yet she would have received more education than most of her female contemporaries. This would, however, have been received from Jutta and by her immersion in the Latin of the regular monastic offices. Jutta (who was groomed for sainthood by the monks) was a crucial formative figure in Hildegard's early life. In *The Life of Hildegard* Godfrey writes of how Jutta carefully introduced her to the habit of humility and innocence, how she taught her the Psalms and showed her how to give praise on her ten-stringed psaltery.

She would not have studied the medieval curriculum – called the *trivuum* – in the systematic way (which consisted largely of rote learning and repetition) of her male contemporaries. It is difficult to know what sort of library the Disibodenberg monastery would have possessed (because of its destruction at the Reformation) or whether Hildegard would have had access to it.

The result of this is that her writing has a uniquely fluid quality which lacks the clarity of contemporary male writers (see Chapter 7). Although her knowledge of the Bible underpins all her work, the references are often oblique and are not clearly set out.

The Magistral Position

At this time, possibly because of the corruption of the church and religious life, there was revival of interest in the hermit life. This looked back to the ideals of the desert fathers and led to men living as roaming hermits and women as enclosed recluses. It led to the vehement resisting of marriage often against parental wishes. This was the story of her mentor, Jutta of Sponheim. Freed from an illness at the age of twelve, Jutta offered her life to God; at twenty she entered into an ascetic life attached to the Abbey of St Disibod, which had been founded in the seventh century, fallen into ruins and in 1108 was starting to be rebuilt. This activity which would have surrounded Hildegard's early life probably produced the tower metaphors of Hildegard's later writing. It is not clear whether the two women worshipped with the monks or had their own chapel. Jutta was, in fact, only six years older than Hildegard and it is possible that the early years of their time together were spent at Sponheim castle where Jutta was being prepared for the spiritual life by Uda von Goellheim.

When Jutta died at forty-four Hildegard was elected leader of the community. At this time there were ten disciples including Hildegard. She now had the services of her faithful friend Volmar, her secretary and probably her confessor, with whom she could share her visions. It is likely that he informed Abbot Kuno of her visions and he relayed the information to the Archbishop of Mainz.

The Visionary

Central to Hildegard's position in her time, when she was known as 'The Sybil of the Rhine', were her visionary experiences. These will be explored in more detail in Chapter 6, but the authority they gave her is central to our understanding of her in the context of her age. Visionaries were much more common then and found a more ready acceptance in an age that could accommodate them theologically more easily than today.

Having received the visions from an early age, she was advised to keep silent about them; but after her mid-life crisis detailed in Chapter 1 she was encouraged to make them public. The visions were accompanied by an illness. This might have been migraine, but many medieval women visionaries experienced illnesses, and it is possible that this was a direct result of the terror induced by the vocation to speak out in a society governed by male authorities both sacred and secular.

Although there is a tradition of visionary experiences in this period, including her contemporary Richard of St Victoire, Hildegard's descriptions of her own visions differ markedly from the traditional distinctions that classified them as imaginative, intellectual and spiritual. Gradually the male visionaries used more of the methods of scholarship and this led to a definition of mysticism which tended to marginalise the more imaginative visions associated with women. Genuine mysticism came to be defined using criteria laid down by the patriarchal authorities.

The conflation of the Old and New Testaments with contemporary issues that characterises her explanations of the visions was born in the practice of *lectio divina* – the meditative study of the Scriptures. This was an important spiritual practice in the Benedictine rule (see Chapter 5), within which was an inbuilt distrust of the dialectical thought being developed at the time in Paris.

Hildegard's claim to being '*indocta*' is significant in her argument for the uniqueness and authority of her visions. As we have seen, she certainly had some education. It is probably an expression of the humility that characterises many medieval visionary texts, like those of Elisabeth of Schoenau, a visionary Benedictine nun at the convent near St Goarshausen on the Rhine, which begins:

> I am a mere poor woman; a vessel of clay. What I say comes not from me but from the clear light: man is a vessel which God fashioned for himself, and filled with his inspiration, so that, in him, he could bring his works to perfection.[2]

A later English mystic, Julian of Norwich. asks readers to ignore her and direct their attention to God, the true author of her vision. What is interesting is that all these mystics give their womanhood as the reason for this. Although the male mystics also point away from themselves towards God, they do not do this on the grounds of their gender.

Hildegard's claim to be unlearned made it absolutely certain that the revelations she received were directly from God. In it lay her claim to be an authentic and authoritative prophetic voice. Slowly this view was confirmed by external authorities. Her earliest extant letter sent in 1147 (and the beginning of what was going to be a vast correspondence involving a wide variety of people) is to Bernard of Clairvaux on the subject of her visions. He was at that moment drumming up support for the Second Crusade:

Reverend Father Bernard, the great honours you have attained through the power of God are a source of wonder; you are truly to be feared by the lawless folly of this world ... Wretched as I am (and more than wretched in bearing the name of woman) I have seen, ever since I was a child, great miracles ... Most true and gentle Father, answer in your goodness, your unworthy maidservant. For never, since I was a child, have I lived an hour free from care. Provide your servant-girl with comfort from your heart.

For in the text, I understand the inner meaning of the exposition of the Psalms and Gospels and the other books which are shown to me by this vision. The vision touches my heart and soul like a burning flame, showing me these depths of interpretation. Yet it does not show me writings in the German tongue – these I do not understand. I only know how to read

the words as a single unit – I cannot pull the text
apart for analysis . . .
Farewell. Be strong in your soul and firm in God's
struggle. Amen.[3]

The reply she received from Bernard is very brief. It
acknowledges that her gift is from God, but stresses
above all that she must be humble. He does not go
into the detail that she is clearly requesting. His reply
is perfunctory and formulaic. However, Bernard was
also present at Trier when Pope Eugene III had parts
of *Scivias* read aloud. After the Pope's affirmation of
Hildegard's authenticity, Bernard became much more
enthusiastic.

The Abbess

Hildegard's acceptance by papal authority and her
increasing fame as a songwriter led to the growth of
her community and in the standing of the Abbey of
Disibodenberg as a whole. However, her dissatisfaction
with her dependence on the male community and the
cramped living conditions led Hildegard with the help
of Henry of Mainz and her important patron, the Marchioness of Stade, to negotiate the purchase of the
Rupertsberg land. This was opposed by the Abbey authorities. Many of the nuns objected to the move initially
but after the establishment of the Rupertsberg, Hildegard affirmed them in words which resemble those of
the opening antiphon.

However, she had to continue to negotiate with the
monks of Disibodenberg. She struggled with them over

the land holdings which had been donated when the nuns were professed. Indeed she was to be dependent on the Abbey of Disibodenberg for the rest of her life. It was only in the thirteenth century that her convent achieved independence.

She also encountered a personal crisis early in her time at the Rupertsberg. Richardis of Stade, daughter of her patron, was an important friend in the Disiboden-berg monastery. She went with Hildegard to the Rupertsberg, but soon was invited by her brother, Arch-bishop Hartwig of Bremen, to accept the post of Abbess at Bassum, near Bremen. This invitation shows how the aristocracy held and controlled ecclesiastical appoint-ments. Hildegard opposed the move and appealed to Pope Eugene to try and stop the appointment. There may even have been an element of jealousy in her oppo-sition as Richardis would have the right to call herself abbess, a title that was not available to Hildegard because her newly founded house was still too closely connected to the monastery of St Disibod. Hildegard wrote a passionate letter to Richardis:

Now, again, I say: Woe is me, your mother, woe is me, daughter – why have you abandoned me like an orphan? I loved the nobility of your conduct, your wisdom and your chastity.

Now let all who have a sorrow like my sorrow mourn with me – all who have ever, in the love of God, had such high love in heart and mind for a human being as I for you – for one snatched away from them in a single moment, as you were from me.

But may the angel of God precede you, and the Son

of God protect you, and his mother guard you. Be mindful of your poor mother Hildegard, that your happiness may not fail.[4]

It is clear that she had a close relationship with Richardis and that this was what later spiritual directors were to call 'a particular friendship'. In the end Richardis was persuaded to return but in 1152, before she had managed this, she died of a fever. Hildegard felt the loss very deeply.

At the Rupertsberg Hildegard would have had the regular round of the Office, the work of the scriptorium in copying books and the organising of provisions for the community as well as for guests and pilgrims. The convent would have provided medical services for all but the very rich. Her medical writings indicate the dedication with which she undertook this work. Guibert of Gembloux describes her later life:

She was assiduous in holy meditation, self-controlled, not wandering in her visions, studious in hearing the holy Scriptures, swift and fearless in elucidating their obscurities, solicitous in observing divine mandates, strenuous in works of mercy, reverent in all things, presumptuous in none, eager in exhorting, effective in persuading and consoling, severe in reprimanding members of her house, temperate in correcting outsiders. She spent sleepless nights singing psalms, closed her ears to slanderers and her detractors, with a heart full of charity and a lamp always bright in work. She was circumspect in speech, sparing in her consumption of food.[5]

Under her supervision the nuns started painting her visions and she completed *Scivias*. The development of her theology of the Virtues (See Chapter 5) is shown in artistic form in *Ordo Virtutum – The Play of the Powers* which was possibly performed at the dedication of the Rupertsberg. This was developed in a new book – *The Book of Life's Merits*.

Her vast correspondence continued and included many letters to religious communities. It was an age of experimentation, including the founding of communities with men and women mixed together and the new order of the Cistercians with its emphasis on manual labour, fasting and poverty and stricter observance of the Benedictine rule. The letters provide an interesting picture of life in the twelfth-century convents and monasteries. In them Hildegard promoted moderate reform and frequently attempted the role of peacemaker. She deals with tired abbots and abbesses wishing to lay down their taxing responsibilities, rivalries for superior positions, impossibly lax or intolerably strict discipline. Many of the letters were combined with actual visits. In all the letters Hildegard's own experience shines through.

She was part of a general movement for the reform of monasticism of the time, but her position in this is not clearly defined. She did not adopt a simple anti-imperial, pro-papal stance but criticised both positions. She was also willing to conceive of institutional reform and commended the Cistercians, although she never considered joining one of the new orders. In her visions she linked the radical changes of her world with those of the New Testament. She believed in the importance of the contemplative life and in it located her hope for ultimate salvation. Her approach was essentially optimistic and as her anticipation of a cataclysm that would befall the church grew, her vision of salvation expanded.

The Preacher

As a preacher and correspondent Hildegard trod a fine political path which allowed her to challenge the various authorities without losing their support. The political scene in which she lived was complex and embraced a number of interlocking issues. Bernard of Clairvaux was mobilising the Second Crusade. There was an ongoing power-struggle between the Holy Roman Empire led by Henry IV and the papacy. Henry wanted control over the appointments of the powerful prince-bishops in the Empire. This brought him into direct conflict with Pope Urban II. This struggle was, in theory, ended by the Concordat of Worms in 1122. The suggested solution was that the bishops would be elected and the pope would invest them with the spiritual regalia, while the emperor could intervene in disputed elections and give them their temporal regalia signifying their feudal role as barons. It was not a secure agreement and the following years saw the emperors trying to control the papacy by raising up anti-popes that they would choose. The popes then retaliated by excommunicating the emperors and raising up anti-kings.

Hildegard was called into one of the most bitter of the disputes by the Emperor Barbarossa who in 1152 asked her to his palace at Ingelheim (not far from the Rupertsberg) to prophesy about his reign. He had vast territorial ambitions and supported the election of three anti-popes starting with Victor IV thus challenging the Pope Alexander III. As the emperor struggled to control the German episcopate, Hildegard became disenchanted with him and warned him against persisting in his divisive policies.

Hildegard endeavoured to give advice to various rulers who sought out her counsel. One such was King Konrad III who had participated in the disastrous Second Crusade on the advice of Pope Eugene and of St Bernard of Clairvaux. When his older son Henry died in 1150, he turned to Hildegard for advice. Her letter is more a prophecy than a direct response:

The One who gives everything life says:

> . . . The justice of God will raise itself up somewhat and the injustice of the clergy and religious will be recognised as thoroughly despicable. And yet no one will dare to raise a sharp and insistent call for repentance. Nevertheless, other times then stand before us: the kindom of the Church will be dissipated; people in clerical and religious life will be torn to pieces as though by a wolf and driven from home and homeland. Very many of them will then move into a kind of solitude, and in deep and heartfelt contrition they will lead a life of poverty and humbly serve God . . .

And again God who knows all things speaks to you, O King: When you hear this, O man, pull yourself together against your self-will and improve yourself so that you may come purified to the times in which you need no more to be ashamed of your days.[6]

In the midst of all this political intrigue, Hildegard developed her own radical solution. In *The Book of Divine Works* she predicted that the papacy would be reduced to the status of a bishopric. By 1174 she had despaired of both papacy and empire. She put forward a visionary solution consisting of a warrior who would look after secular government, and a group of prophets to look after spiritual affairs. She did not favour a single figure in charge of both church and state and saw the prophets as supporting the renewal which the hero-king would instigate.

In the church there was increasing centralisation of power. Hildegard saw the need for a pope of true integrity. In her letter to Pope Anastasius IV (who was in office 1153–4 and had tolerated corrupt men in positions of authority), she reminds him of his high calling:

So it is, O man, that you who sit in the chief seat of the Lord, hold him in contempt when you embrace evil, since you do not reject it but kiss it, by silently tolerating it in depraved men . . .

Now listen to him who lives and will not be destroyed. The world at this time is steeped in wantonness; after this, it will be in sadness; then in terror, so that people will not be concerned if they are killed . . . But the heart will save, when the dawn will appear with the splendour of the first sunrise. But what follows in the new desire, in the new zeal, is beyond utterance.[7]

There was also a great drive towards the conversion

of laity. The church wanted to take control of marriage away from parents by making it a sacrament administered under canon law. The development of a pastoral system included the formalisation of the practice of sacramental confession. Parts of Hildegard's *Book of Life's Merits* would seem to be part of this movement giving advice on recommended remedies like prayer and fasting and some quite severe penances. Among the many letters written to clergy and religious communities, she wrote this letter to Christian lay people that reminds us of the antiphon at the opening of this chapter:

> All of you people who were born and cleansed through God's wisdom, hear what I, the radiant light and Creator of all of you, have to say to you. You were planted in My heart at daybreak on the first day of creation . . . Why do you forget the One who has created you and given you everything! When God gives you what is necessary, God does it in such a way that sometimes allows you certain things and sometimes does not.[8]

By this time Hildegard was working on *The Book of Divine Works*. It is her most developed piece of theology and contains passages like the following, mercilessly attacking the failings of the clergy:

> How long will we suffer and endure these ravening wolves, who ought to be physicians and are not?
> And how can it be right that the shaven-headed with their robes and chasubles should have more soldiers and more weapons than we do? Surely too,

it is inappropriate for a cleric to be a soldier or a soldier a cleric? So let us take away from them what is not fairly but unjustly theirs . . .

For the Almighty Father has rightly divided all things . . . God indeed has not decreed that the tunic and cloak should be given to one son while the other remains naked, but has ordered that the cloak should be given to one, the tunic to the other. And so let the laity have the cloak, because of the bulk of their worldly concerns and on account of their offspring who are always growing and multiplying. But let the tunic be given to the religious population, so that they lack neither food nor clothing, but do not possess more than they need.[9]

This is powerful writing, not designed to endear her to the local clergy. What is surprising is that these same priests, far from decrying her authority actually invited her to preach and afterwards asked for copies of her sermons. It is not clear whether she preached in Latin or German, as the transcripts of sermons were tradition-ally in Latin, whatever language they had been preached in originally.

Like the contemporary visionary Elisabeth of Scho-enau, she supported the church authorities in their struggle with the Cathars, a sect that grew up as the antithesis to the laxity of the clerics. The clergy were taking concubines, bishoprics were bought and sold and the greed of the priests and bishops meant they neglected the care of their congregations, as she identified in the letter cited above. The Cathars developed a dualistic doctrine, renouncing the material world, favouring a vegetarian diet, abstaining from sexual relations and often ending up with self-starvation. In *Scivias* she stressed the importance of marriage, the centrality of the eucharist and the significance of the priesthood, the very doctrines that the Cathars denied.

She conducted four preaching tours after the age of sixty, beginning in 1158. For the first three she travelled largely by boat on the rivers Main, Moselle and Rhine. The last, overland to Swabia, was the most difficult and was undertaken when she was well into her seventies.

Hildegard's development of the figure of Ecclesia in her visionary experiences shows her sadness at the situation in the church, especially when she is portrayed with scaly spots and a foul black head in her vagina (see Chapter 5). This contrasts sharply with male writers of her day such as Rupert of Deutz who, like Hildegard, was a reformer brought up in a conservative Benedictine tradition, but believed that the church would remain strong, set against the secular authorities. The church would be a bulwark against the Anti-Christ. For Hildegard, however, it would only be a faithful remnant of the character described in the opening antiphon, not the institutional church, that would provide such a bulwark. She saw the church itself as giving birth to the Anti-Christ. She foresaw that the church's properties would be confiscated, but a faithful group would live humbly in solitude and a purified clergy would return the church to its early state at the 'first dawn of justice'. It is to this chosen 'elect' that the antiphon at the opening of the chapter refers.

The Holy Woman

Hildegard's reputation became well established. By the mid–1160s she had founded a second house at Eibingen on the other side of the Rhine possibly for nuns of less aristocratic origins. She visited this by boat twice a week and local people gathered on the shore to ask for her assistance. Sick people like the young woman Sigewize who was possessed by a devil were sent to her for help (see Chapter 7).

In 1173, in the middle of the revision of *The Book of Divine Works*, Volmar her secretary died. This was not only a personal loss, but also made it necessary for her to negotiate again with the Abbot of Disibodenberg for a monk to act as provost to her community. All women's communities needed a priest and confessor but as she grew older with a growing community Hildegard needed administrative and secretarial help as well. In the end, she was given Godfrey who embarked on writing her *Life*.

Her continued challenge to the church may have led her in her final year to fall foul of the canons at Mainz. She would have acquired some of her income at the Rupertsberg from the burial of the dead of local families in the convent grounds. In 1178, she agreed to the burial of a nobleman who had been excommunicated. Witnesses proved that he had been reconciled to the church before his death and had received the last rites. The canons apparently did not know about or accept this, and imposed on Hildegard and her community a collective excommunication, which meant that they could not receive communion and had to whisper rather than sing

the office. It is possible that the canons had a grievance
against the nobleman. It is interesting to speculate on
why Hildegard was prepared to make this stand. Maybe
she had counselled the nobleman's family and was aware
of the effects of unresolved issues around a death. She
penned the skilful letter referred to in her story and
printed in Chapter 7 setting out the theology of music.
This and the intervention of her friend Archbishop Philip
of Cologne who testified to the dead man's confession
secured the lifting of the interdict.

Reputation

Hildegard's story is one of growing recognition of her
authority. She spread her message widely using a variety
of methods – letters, preaching tours and her writings.
Her reputation after her death was secured by the production in 1220 of *The Mirror of Future Times*, a digest
of the apocalyptic passages from her visions, produced
by the monk Gebeno of Eberbach.

There are many extant letters from her admirers. The
dean and clergy of Cologne called her the 'very oracle
of God'. Guibert of Gembloux described her as 'a new
Mary bringing forth the word of God'. The monks of
Haina addressed her as the 'chosen and beloved spouse
of the highest king and a lantern burning for the illumination of the church'.

The process of canonisation was never successfully
completed. Her supporters were hopeful, especially as
Pope Alexander II was still reigning at the time of her
death. Her manuscripts were produced in finely decorated forms, pilgrimages were encouraged to her shrine,

the miracles were documented, music was composed for her feast day and an altarcloth embroidered depicting her as a saint.

However, the proceedings were not officially opened until 1227 when Pope Alexander was dead and few remained who remembered her miracles. Despite the support of Pope Gregory IX, the bureaucratic processes were not successfully negotiated. The trend in the thirteenth century was away from the established orders of the Benedictines in favour of the new orders such as the Dominicans and Franciscans and lay women associated with these orders. In popular practice she was regarded as a saint and her cult increased. In 1940 the Vatican approved the celebration of her feast day in Germany. Moves are underway today to have her accepted as a 'doctor of the church' like Teresa of Avila and Catherine of Siena.

The Bingen house was destroyed by the Swedes in 1632 during the Thirty Years War. The Eibingen house was dissolved in 1814 as the Napoleonic era increased secularisation. It was refounded in 1907 and exists today as a centre for scholarly research into Hildegard.

Exercise

Hildegard's letters have a confidence based on her theological view of politics. She reminds those in authority of their vocation. Examine current situations in newspapers, in media broadcasts or on the internet. Select a situation that you feel particularly strongly about it. Think about the demands of justice in that situation. Try to envisage that justice in the context of God's plan for the salvation of the cosmos. Imagine yourself in it in your meditation time. See how God is speaking in it and through it.

Write a letter to one of the people who has power in that situation suggesting a course of action set in a theological context.

3

JUSTICE AND INTERRELATIONSHIP

Antiphon: Aer enim volat

For air flows freely
And serves every part of creation.
That is its real duty and function.
The firmament is sustained within it,
And air itself is also nourished by that same power.[1]

In her theology Hildegard is a traditionalist. Her first work *Scivias* is set within the context of the church's teaching in the twelfth century, as she elaborates the overarching plan of a transcendent God from creation to redemption. Yet to this scheme she brought her own unique vision. She lived in an age when the interconnectedness of all knowledge had not been broken up. For her the cosmos was an interdependent organism in which the elements of the natural world, the angels, human beings and God are in indivisible relationship (see Chapter 7). For Hildegard relationship was central.

The Image of the Wheel

Hildegard used the image of the wheel to express this unity. In the *Book of Divine Works* she wrote:

The Trinity in the Unity

The Godhead is like a wheel, a whole. In no way is it to be divided . . . Every creature is linked to another and every essence is constrained by another.[2]

The image is explained most fully at the opening of *Causes and Cures* (see Chapter 8):

God remained complete like a wheel, and he remained the father in goodness, for his fatherhood is filled with his goodness. And so this fatherhood is very just, very kind, very stable, and very strong . . . The rim of the wheel is fatherhood, the fullness of the wheel is divinity. Everything is within it and stems from it, and there is no creator beyond. Lucifer on the other hand, is not whole but is divided and scattered, because he wanted to be what he should not be. For when God made the world, he had already determined in his ancient plan that he wanted to become human.[3]

All of creation is included within the wheel. Creation contains within it the plan for incarnation. Human beings and the divine are thus inextricably intertwined.

The paintings of her visions are often set in shapes like circles or ovals that emphasise relatedness; others are in the form of large figures containing smaller figures (see Chapter 6). In the second vision of *Scivias*, she sees the Trinity in circular form. Her description is simple and striking:

Then I saw a bright light, and in this light the figure of a man the colour of sapphire, which was all blazing with a gentle glowing fire. And that bright light bathed the whole of the glowing fire, and the glowing fire bathed the bright light; and the bright light and the glowing fire poured over the whole human figure, so that the three were one light in one power of potential.[4]

In her explanation, the bright light represents the Father; the man in sapphire blue is the Son and the gently glowing fire, the Holy Spirit. The whole represents the inseparability of the Trinity.

Justice as Interrelationship

For Hildegard the essence of goodness is right connection. In *The Book of Divine Works* she develops her idea that God and the cosmos necessarily have the same shape – a circle; for the creation perfectly reflects the Creator and creation and incarnation are inextricably connected. For her the notion of sin was one of a break in this relationship, as can be seen in the second vision of the first book of *Scivias* (see Chapter 6). In a dramatic picture Adam is portrayed as falling from Paradise into a fiery pit at the instigation of Lucifer. In the corners of the vision are the four elements (a characteristic of many of her visions). In her explanation she sets out the beauty of the interrelatedness of the garden as God set it out. Lucifer's crime intrudes on the unity of this garden causing it to lose its balance and its natural wholeness:

All the elements of the world, which before had existed in great calm, were turned to the greatest agitation and displayed horrible terrors.[5]

She relates this to the human condition. Because Adam has made God angry, the elements are now against him. As the elements are inside Adam as well as outside, he is now unbalanced and falls into the chasm. So the goal of salvation is the restoration of the interconnectedness that was lost. Through redemption the creation will once again perfectly reflect the Creator.

Eve is represented as a cloud coming from Adam's side. In it is an array of bright stars. These represent the whole human race including Jesus which she carries within herself. So within her is the possibility of the redemption of the Fall. So the Fall and the redemption are inextricably intertwined.

Dualistic Theology

In line with this cosmic theology Hildegard treated the dualisms that characterised her age as being in continual relationship. She revisited oppositions such as dark/light, good/evil and body/soul. For her, the negative was always in relationship with the positive. This runs through all her writing and is typified by the following quotations:

> Human beings fly with two wings; the right wing is the knowledge of good and the left is the knowledge of evil. The knowledge of evil serves the good insofar as the good is sharpened and highlighted through the knowledge of evil; and so through this knowledge human beings become wise in all things.[6]

This has implications for the way in which we live our lives:

Use all your faculties to appreciate God's creation. Use your soul to understand other souls. Use your body to sympathise with other people's bodily experiences. Use your emotions of anger and revenge to understand war. Appreciate goodness through distinguishing it from evil. Appreciate beauty through distinguishing it from ugliness and deformity. Define poverty by contrasting it with wealth. Rejoice in good health by comparing it with sickness. Distinguish the various opposites: length and shortness; hardness and softness; depth and shallowness; light and darkness. Enjoy every moment of life by constantly reminding yourself of the imminence of death. Look forward to paradise by reminding yourself of eternal punishment. You understand so little of what is around you because you do not use what is within you.[7]

This reflects clearly how she perceived the relationship between the soul and the body. Her work can be seen as anticipating a redemption of the role of the body as seen in the negative tradition of some of the church fathers.

Vision four of the first book of *Scivias* contains the striking image of the soul being infused into the womb of a pregnant woman (see Chapters 4 and 7). In explaining the vision Hildegard wrestles with these ideas:

The soul now shows its powers according to the powers of the body, so that in a person's infancy is produces simplicity, in his youth strength, and in adulthood, when all the person's veins are full, it shows its strongest powers in wisdom; as the tree in its first shoots is tender and then shows that it can bear fruit, and finally, in its full utility, bears it. But then in human old age, when the marrow and veins start to incline to weakness, the soul's powers are gentler, as if from a weariness at human knowledge; as when winter approaches the sap of the tree diminishes in the branches and the leaves, and the tree in its old age begins to bend.[8]

A tension between body and soul continues in her writing. In her *Life* she wrestles with relating it to the Old and New Testaments:

In a genuine vision, I saw the condition of mankind. Although human beings by nature are composed of body and soul, they are nonetheless a single structure; similarly, the person who is constructing a building of stone covers and fastens together the various materials so that the house does not fall apart. A human being is the work of God. He is with all creatures, and every creature is with him. However, the work of a human being, which is without life, is unlike the work of God, which is life, just as the work of the potter has no similarity with the works of the blacksmith. The nature of the soul is truly made for everlasting life; the body on the other hand has a corruptible life. But the two are not superimposed one on the other. Although they are found together at the same time in a person, they are nevertheless different from one another.[9]

The Role of Art in Cosmic Order

Music played a significant role in the process of connection, the redemption of lost and wrong connection (see Chapter 8). Hildegard's music flows forward in a continuous stream. Because the words and music were given to her together, her poetry has a similar pattern. The texts of her songs are characterised by the use of many conjunctions, which is reflected in the free flowing nature of the musical setting:

> O wound flowing with blood
> That cries aloud to the highest,
> When all elemental forces
> Are themselves entangled
> And crying with lamenting voice
> Bringing terror,
> Because this is the blood of creation itself touching
>   them,
> Anoint us
> So that our wounds may be healed.[10]

In this single sentence, the ideas pour forth in a connected stream that adds to the song's immediacy and reveals the clear connectedness of the thought behind it. This is crucial to Hildegard's theology. Our wounds are intrinsically bound up with the cosmic cataclysm that has produced the 'wound flowing with blood'. These features reflect the free-flowing interconnectedness of her thought patterns which in turn reflect those of the universe. The piling up of clause upon clause gives the poetry a cumulative power. Her prose writing is similar containing interjections like Why? and How? which give it the quality of the free flowing of speech rather than the more statuesque quality of traditional prose.

Compassion

Her notion of connectedness leads us to both an appreciation of compassion for the cosmos and a passion for justice. These two are sometimes difficult to balance. It is the dilemma of when to speak out and when to keep silent that Hildegard faced throughout her life. It is the dilemma of having understanding for the oppressor and yet challenging the oppression itself.

Exercises

1. Imagine yourself in the very centre of the image of The Trinity in the Unity (p. 32). Imagine a spot on the top of your head opening up to the universe. Feel the strength of the universe flowing into you. Feel the connection with *viriditas*, the life-giving power of God.
2. Reflect on a natural disaster that has happened recently. Imagine the devastation and the human suffering. Avoid trying to work out why it happened but imagine the whole scene held in God's love and the human beings and the natural world restored in their relationship. After the reflection see what you personally could do to help further this process.
3. Find a beautiful object to contemplate or recall a

situation in which you have felt real peace or happiness. Try writing an account as a long stream of consciousness without censoring what you are writing. It may help to do it as if you were telling someone about it or to record it on a tape and transcribe it. When you have finished look at your use of connecting words. See if you can introduce more so that the piece rushes to a climax at the end.

4. Create a personal ceremony concerned with right relationship with a group of friends. Get each person to bring an object that for them represents justice and ecology. Arrange them in relation within a circular sacred space. Here are some of the elements you might use:

For the creation of a sacred space:
Grant O God your protection and in your protection strength
And in your strength understanding and in your understanding to know justice
And in knowing justice to love wisely and in loving the whole created world wisely to love God.

Based on an ancient Celtic prayer

Use objects like stones or twigs or flowers for intercession. Have a pile of them somewhere in the circle and as you pray for a situation or person place them one by one in a bowl.

You might like to use this contemporary hymn which can be sung to Abbots Leigh (usually used for *Glorious things of thee are spoken*):

1. God of justice, wind the circle,
   Making all the cosmos one,
   Show us in millennial visions,
   How on earth your will is done;
   Help us see the mercy flowing
   From the wounding of Christ's side;
   Heal us with compassion spreading
   As a purifying tide.

2. God of dreams and intuition
   Inspiration from the night,
   Temper reason's rigid systems
   With the leap of faith's insight.
   God of passion, fill our knowing
   With divine authority
   And a sense of mystery leading
   To a right humility.

3. God of faith's heroic journey,
   May your truth direct our way;
   Guide our footsteps, give us courage
   In the challenge of each day.
   God of wisdom's spinning spiral,
   Soothe us with your gentle charms
   Weave our lives into the pattern
   Of Christ's all-embracing arms.

4. God of order, God of chaos,
    In love's creativity
    Move the mountains of tradition
    Stifling earth's fertility;
    Break the barriers, guide the learning,
    Bind the wounds and heal the pain;
    Bring to birth our human yearning,
    Integrate the world again.

4

PRAYER IN COMMUNITY

Antiphon: O pastor animarum

> O Counsellor of all souls
> And O Primal Voice
> Which called all of us into being,
> We are praying to you, to you,
> That in your strength
> We may find freedom from our misery
> And our general weakness[1]

Hildegard left no manual of prayer and no guides or hints on how to achieve states of ecstasy. We can only construe her own practice from her writings and visionary experiences and her rootedness in the Benedictine tradition.

God the Counsellor

The image of God as a heavenly counsellor in the opening antiphon could be seen as rooted in Hildegard's own experience of lostness. She was oblated at the age of eight in what might well have been quite a frightening ceremony. In *Scivias* she rails against the practice of child oblature. This is in the context of her exposition of her vision of Ecclesia (see Chapter 5). The oratory becomes very impassioned at this point, reflecting the strength of Hildegard's feeling about her own oblature:

And how did you dare so rashly to touch one dedicated and sanctified so that without his will you handed him over to bear My yoke in strict captivity; so that he became neither dry nor green, not dying to the world or living to the world? Why have you so oppressed him that he can do neither? If I comfort him by miracle so that he remain in the spiritual life, that is not for humans to look into; for I want his parents not to sin in his oblation, offering him to Me without his will.

But if anyone, father or mother, wishes to offer their child to My service let them say before presenting him, 'I promise God that I will keep my child with skilful care until he reaches the age of reason, entreating, beseeching and exhorting him to go permanently into God's service. And if he says yes, I will speedily offer him to the service of God; but if he does not consent, may I be guiltless in the sight of God's Majesty.'[2]

In her fantasy based on Hildegard's writings Ingeborg Ulrich expands this into an imaginative story:

She hears her parents talking. She must leave home . . . She is still small, only eight years old. Her mother insists. Her father hesitates: he is afraid it is too soon, it might hurt her. They talk about tithing, about obligation . . . rarely has her mother talked so much. Why did her father not offer a powerful rebuttal?[3]

In a community pageant based on Hildegard's life, one of the most moving moments was when the young child turned to wave a long goodbye to her parents before entering Jutta's house. It is a theme I have explored in my opera, *A Life Apart*. In this, in an impassioned outburst, Hildegard remembers how her parents abandoned her and examines her lost childhood. In one of the few moments when she speaks she says: 'All my life I have looked for little Hildegard.'[4]

The Lost Child and Comforting Figures

It is not by accident that this statement about the abandonment of children is contained in her exposition of one of the large female figures that dominate her visions. Returning to the vision she includes a speech in which the soul laments her lostness:

> Oh, where am I? Ach, from whence did I come here? And what comforter shall I seek in this captivity? How shall I break these chains? Oh, what eye can look on my wounds? And what nose can bear their loathsome stench? And what hands will anoint them with oil? Oh who will console me, since even my mother has abandoned me since I strayed from the path of salvation? Who will help me but God?[5]

The soul in this vision passes through a number of difficult experiences of grief and sorrow, where she appears to find her mother and then loses her again and again. In her isolation she is exposed to scorpions and serpents.

> Terrified I uttered the loudest of shrieks, crying. 'O mother, where are you? I would suffer less if I had not lately felt the sweetness of your presence . . . And

then I heard my mother's voice, saying to me 'O daughter, run! For the Most Powerful Giver whom no one can resist has given you wings to fly with.'[6]

As always in her writings she draws on a variety of biblical images including the suffering and grief of Jeremiah and Job, the wandering of Israel in the wilderness, Elijah's experience in the cave and the women in Revelation chapter 12. She finds comfort from a number of female images.

It is possible to see how in God (especially in the female images) Hildegard found her lost mother. The antiphon at the beginning of this chapter shows a compassionate, strengthening God who delivers human beings from their weakness. In *A Life Apart*[7] I present her devotion to the Virgin Mary as a particularly strengthening one. Hildegard offers her scarred heart to Mary after the end of the relationship with Richardis (see pp 18–19) and although the virginity of Mary is central to her own vow of chastity, Mary's motherhood is also an important theme.

Life in Community

Jutta of Sponheim, the anchoress with whom Hildegard lived in those early days at Disibodenberg must also have become like a mother to her. In founding her own community at the Rupertsberg, Hildegard may be seen as making for herself a new family to replace the one that she had lost so early in life. The pattern of collaborative and communal living and prayer gave her both an earthly and a heavenly family.

She put her own distinctive stamp upon it. The *lingua ignota*, a language with an alphabet of twenty-three letters and containing nine hundred nouns (referring to clothes worn by the nuns, garden herbs and a range of mystical beings), may well have originated as a secret language for her chosen sisters. It could be seen as carrying the mystical aspirations of the community and keeping it protected from the outside world which might misunderstand or attack it. There may have been other reasons for this as well – a medicinal code, a game of some kind or a language delighting in purely sensuous sounds.

The community also gave Hildegard a chance to explore the creation of artistic works – poetry, music, drama, dance, liturgy. This was an age when art was still contextualised, so everything she created was in the context of the provision of regular material for the liturgy (see Chapter 8). Here she could share her visionary experiences immediately with a wider community.

Collaboration

Hildegard also conceived of the receiving of her visions and her creative work in a collaborative way, working with both Richardis of Stade and Volmar. This is clear in an illustration from the Lucca manuscript of *The Book of Divine Works* in which Hildegard receives her visions as a stream of heavenly light and writes them on to a tablet. The nun standing behind her is thought to be Richardis. On the other side of a grille Volmar is taking down the words from dictation and editing them. Richardis and Volmar are portrayed as collaborators,

Hildegard receives her visions

fulfilling the divine vocation to record and tell what they have seen and heard.

Hildegard's position is typical of medieval and especially Anglo-Saxon and Romanesque author portraits, in that she faces forward, leans to the left and bends over her writing equipment. However, in other ways it is different. First, this is the only illustration of a woman

visionary and its creation must have required considerable courage on her part. Male visionaries could link
their experience with one of the four evangelists. The
streaming light from heaven replaces the more usual
symbols of a dove for the Spirit, the hand of God or an
evangelist's trumpet. The presence of Volmar with note-
pad at the ready is also unusual. An evangelist-author is
typically portrayed alone. Hildegard is contained in a cell-
like surround and the whole is enclosed in a monastic type
building. Her visions are seen in the context of a monastic
community and in association with a male adviser. She
chooses to portray herself not as an isolated visionary but
as a woman deeply rooted in the monastic tradition.
Her mysticism involves collaboration. It made the loss
of Richardis even more difficult and the theme of abandonment runs through the letters to Richardis.

Benedictine Spirituality

Hildegard founded her order on the Rule of Benedict.
She would have celebrated the Offices seven times a day,
according to the ancient pattern:

> Sometime before sunrise: Matins
> At dawn: Lauds
> Around 6 a.m.: Prime
> Around 9 a.m.: Terce (which would have been fol-
>   lowed by the Mass)
> At noon: Sext
> At 3 p.m.: None
> At sunset: Vespers
> Before bed: Compline

Central to the Rule was the notion of communality. Benedictine religious claimed no dominion over their wills or their bodies. There was no personal ownership of property and no privacy. Meals and work were communal experiences and the day was organised around a three-hourly communal prayer cycle even through the night. This rhythm underpinned Hildegard's thinking. There was a struggle when she moved from her more cloistered life before the vision at the age of forty-three into a more public life at the Rupertsberg. Not only did this mean revealing the nature of her visions (see Chapter 6) but exchanging the private life of an anchoress for a life in the public gaze. She became an active nun, out in the world, preaching and teaching and in touch with people in order to heal them.

Guibert of Gembloux praises life at the Rupertsberg:

Here there is a wonderful competition among virtues. The mother embraces her daughters with such love, and the daughters submit to the mother with such reverence, that one can scarcely distinguish whether in this fervour the mother outstrips the daughters or vice versa. Mindful of the invitation of the Lord, 'Be still and see that I am God,' on feast days they abstain from work, sitting in silence in their seclusion, and dedicate themselves with zeal to reading and to learning songs. And obedient to the words of the Apostle, 'whoever does not work, shall not eat', they busy themselves in their own rooms on workdays by copying from books and by producing liturgical garments or other handcrafts.

Moreover, this cloister is not something founded

by an emperor or bishop or some powerful or rich person of this earth but by a poor, involved, weak woman. Within this short time, about twenty-seven years, the true monastic spirit as well as the external buildings were so highly developed that everything was in good working order – not in ostentatious but in stately and roomy buildings – which were befitting nuns – and in all the workrooms there was running water. Expenses were adequately covered not only for the many guests which were never lacking in the house of God and the various employees of which there was a great number, but also for clothing and sustenance for about fifty sisters.

The one who is mother and leader of such a large complex is lavish in her love for all. She gives counsel when requested, solves difficult questions which are put to her, writes books, instructs her sisters, puts a fresh heart into sinners who come to her, and is fully and entirely busy with everything. In spite of the burden of age and sickness, she accomplished so much by the exercise of all the virtues that she could say with the Apostle Paul, for example, 'I have become all things to win all people', and 'I will rather boast most gladly of my weaknesses in order that the power of Christ may dwell with me; for when I am weak, then I am strong.' (2 Cor. 12:9)[8]

In her beautiful fictional meditational account of Hildegard's life, Ingeborg Ulrich suggests that Hildegard was uncomfortable with some of the harsher aspects of the Benedictine Rule. Her more gentle counselling comes from the Counsellor God of the opening antiphon:

At the end of Compline there is a shriek. Reingard tears the veil from her head, rips off the bands, shakes her head back and forth, strikes it against the bench ... Hildegard goes into the kitchen. The fire in the stove has already been covered. The wind is in the chimney. It takes some time before she can kindle the fire; she is not skilled in these things ... Prayers lie between her lips. Then she goes to Reinhard ... releases the fetters on her shoulders and breast. Her face is grotesque. Hildegard knows what is wrong. She is silent. She supports the other woman's head. Drink. She administers lavender, myrrh, dill, puts the cup to her mouth, takes it away, is silent, holds her head, gives the cup again. Her breath is quieter, her features soften. Drink. The rule prescribes punishments, but Hildegard knows better. Be silent, put the cup aside, lay the head on the coverlet, stroke the left arm toward the heart, softly, slowly. Like the dew of Hermon which falls on the mountains of Zion.[9]

Lectio Divina

The reading of Scripture is a central part of the Benedictine Rule. The Scriptures would have been read aloud during meals as well as forming a significant part of the regular Offices. The purpose of this was to allow the Word of God to dwell in the human heart richly. Phrases would be remembered and repeated regularly so that they became an intrinsic part of the person. This is a process of incarnation in the life of the individual soul. It is very different from the contemporary notion of reading for intellectual understanding. Hildegard's

visions are filled with scriptural references which reflect
how well she practised *lectio divina*.

The Role of the Body in Prayer

Hildegard's spirituality is rooted in the everyday. She
writes that holy people draw to themselves everything
that is earthly. She uses very domestic images. Her
images of the Spirit (see Chapter 10) draw on all sorts
of practical images like perfumes and infusions and tight
fitting garments.

A favourite image of praying involves the very bodily
image of sweating using the verb *sudare*:

> Flowing in and out like the breath, the marrow of the
> hip sweats its essence, carrying and strengthening the
> person. In just such a manner the vitality of earth's
> elements comes from the strength of the Creator. It is
> this vigour that hugs the world: warming, moistening,
> firming, greening. This is so that all creatures might
> germinate and grow.
>
> When in the fullness of its time this creation wilts,
> its vigour returns to its own source. This is the under-
> lying natural law. When the elements of the world
> fulfil their function, they come to ripeness and their
> fruit is gathered back to God. Now these things are
> in reference to the soul's life: spirituality is alive in
> the soul in the same way as the marrow of the hips
> in the flesh. Out of the soul in good standing, the
> vigour of the virtues flows out as do the elements of
> creation, it flows back in the same capacity in attentive
> prayer.[10]

There are indications that her community were encouraged to wear clothing that reflected divine beauty, suitable for Brides of Christ. As the secular wife adorns herself for her husband so should the monastic virgin be beautifully dressed in her love for her heavenly Bridegroom. On holy days they wore white veils, tiaras with gems and rings on their fingers. She described the symbolism of the garments her nuns wore, following the figures in her visions. The white veil signified the radiant robes of Paradise, and the three-coloured circlet on their heads, the Trinity. The robes may have been based on the costumes for the Virtues in the music drama *Ordo Virtutum* (see Chapter 8) that were then used as part of monastic life.

Exercises

1. Imagine some aspect of your life that you feel was chosen for you rather than by you. Reflect prayerfully upon it and see if there is any act that you can undertake to make the decision your own or to renounce the decision.

Pray for all children separated from or abused by their parents. You may like to use Hildegard's responsory for the innocents:

> God responds speedily
> When the blood of innocence is being shed
> Of this the Angel choirs are singing
> And re-echoing their praise,

And yet at the loss of innocence clouds are
    weeping.

2. Remember a time when you felt lost and abandoned. Imagine God meeting you in that experience
and surrounding you with love. Recall the form that
God takes in this visualisation and try to retain it
in the form of an image or a phrase that you can use
in future times of difficulty.
3. Think of a situation or a person that needs something beautiful. It can be a work of art, a song, or
tune, an item of delicious food or a flower arrange-
ment. Imagine what your offering could do for the
situation and then set about making it prayerfully,
mindfully bringing love into that situation.
4. Imagine yourself surrounded by a net of praying
people – picture your own place in it, or resting in
it like a hammock. Whose praying hammocks would
you also be part of? Who do you pray for?

5

WISDOM AND THE VIRGIN MARY

Antiphon: O frondens virga

O green leafy branch,
In your nobility you stand;
Just like the dawn you bear rich fruit.
Now you can rejoice and sing.
Give dignity when we are weak;
Set us free from ways of living that keep us trapped;
Also empower us with your strong arm
To live life to the full.[1]

Wisdom

We have seen in the previous chapter how Hildegard's loss of her mother early in her life might have influenced her development of a theology of the Virgin. The opening antiphon to the Virgin Mary likens her to a green, leafy branch that can empower us. From her she develops a number of female figures. This theology is based on Wisdom traditions of the Old Testament and in this she sits within a long line of sapiential (Wisdom) theologians that include Joseph Trimethius (1462–1516), Jakob Boehme (1575–1624), Ann Lee, founder of the Shakers, the Russian Vladimir Soloviev (1853–

1900) and the twentieth-century Catholic theologian, Pierre Teilhard de Chardin. Her concept of the feminine in God is therefore not a break with tradition but rather a rediscovery of a more ancient tradition.

In *Scivias* the figure of Wisdom/Sapientia is developed. In Book Three, vision four she is portrayed inside a three-sided pillar, crowned with a radiant dove. The three sides represent the patriarchs and prophets who showed forth the ancient Law, the new life of grace in apostles, martyrs and virgins and the wisdom of the doctors. Wisdom is identified as *Scientia Dei* (Knowledge of God) and is veiled because she is too bright and glorious to look at – a paradoxical figure embodying both terror and tenderness. She has a human form and is surrounded by angels and human beings venerating her. She is surveying the people who have come into the building and are putting on new garments, saying to each:

> Consider the garment you have put on, and do not forget the Creator who made you.[2]

The Dance at the Heart of the World

Wisdom points to the Creator and acts as a co-creator with him. She mediates between God and creation. By incarnating in humans she makes them co-responsible with God in creating the universe. In the ninth vision of Book Three of *Scivias* she appears in a striking form which brings together these aspects (the vision itself is in italics):

You see a figure of great beauty standing on the top of this floor. This means that this virtue was in the Father on high 'before all creation', arranging in his judgement all the materials of creation established in heaven and on earth. She herself, it is clear, shines in him as a great adornment, being the broadest step amongst the steps of the other virtues in him. She is joined to him in a dance, in the sweetest embrace of blazing love.

Wisdom looks towards the people on the earth. For she always rules and defends with her protection those who try to follow her, loving them greatly because they are steadfast in her. For that same figure signifies the Wisdom of God: since, through her, all things were created and are ruled by God. *Her head shines like lightning: with such brightness that you cannot have your fill of gazing upon it.* For the Godhead is both terrible and enticing to all creation, seeing and contemplating all things, just as the human eye discerns what is placed before it. Yet no mortal can ultimately comprehend the Godhead, in all the profundity of its mystery.

Wisdom arranges her hands reverently upon her breast. This signifies the power of Wisdom which she wisely restrains, so that she directs every work of hers in such a way that no one can resist her, either in prudence or power.

Her feet on the same floor, are hidden from Your sight. For her way, concealed in the heart of the Father, lies open to no mortal. Her secrets are naked and manifest to God alone. *She has on her head a ring in the form of a crown, shining with great brilli-*

ance. This signifies that the majesty of God, being without beginning or end, shines with an incomparable glory, Godhead radiating with such splendour that mortal minds are overwhelmed. As for her being clothed in a tunic the colour of gold; this signifies that the work of Wisdom is frequently considered as though it were the purest gold. For this reason, *she is adorned with a belt that descends from her breast right down to her feet, decorated with most precious jewels and glittering in a brilliant play of green and white and red and sky-blue.* For, from the beginning of the world, like a single path, adorned with holy and just commands, that is to say, with the first planting of the green seed of the patriarchs and of the prophet . . . Then she was graced with the dazzling virginity of the Virgin Mary; next, with the solid and ruddy faith of the martyrs; and finally with the brilliant and light-filled love of contemplation, by which God and neighbours ought to be loved through the heat of the Holy Spirit.

She will go on in this way until the end of the world, and her warning will not cease but will flow out always, as long as the world endures.[3]

In the ninth vision of *The Book of Divine Works*, Wisdom is seen as beyond human reason. She is likened to a glowing jewel. She wears a green cloak and is thus linked with the concept of *viriditas*, the greening power at the heart of the universe (see Chapter 10). Human beings are exhorted to put on her garment through good intentions and deeds.

The Virtues

The Virtues are seen as feminine figures emanating from Wisdom. The Latin word *virtus* has within it also a sense of strength, energy and power. Hildegard develops them in her three theological books as divine qualities that operate within co-operative human souls. They represent the feminine synergy between humanity and divinity in which the divine plan for salvation is worked out. They appear early in *Scivias* featuring in the magnificent Vision of the Choirs of Angels (see Chapter 8):

> These are the Virtues, which spring up in the hearts of believers, and in ardent charity build in them a lofty tower, which is their works; so that in their reason they show the deeds of the elect, and in their strength they bring them to a good end with great glory of blessedness.[4]

Here they form a vital link between the work of God within the souls of believers and its expression in good works. They feature prominently in the musical morality play *Ordo Virtutum* (which is variously translated as *The Play of the Virtues* or *The Play of the Powers*) where they represent the protectors of the soul against the wiles of the Devil and a powerful army that in the end defeats him. They are most carefully worked out in *The Book of Life's Merits* where each virtue is set against its corresponding vice. Vices appear as twisted, mangled forms of the virtues.

Hildegard becomes taken up with the figure of Caritas

– Love. In *The Book of Life's Merits* Caritas responds
to her twisted form, the vice Envy:

> Oh most filthy filth, you are like a snake that attacks
> itself, for you cannot sustain anything that is stable
> and honourable . . . I, however, am the air, I nourish
> all greenness and bring flowers to mature fruit . . . I
> bring forth tears from a good sigh as I also bring forth
> a good aroma from tears through most holy works.
> I am also the rain that rises from the dew through
> which the grass rejoices with rich life. You, however,
> the most wicked and worst poison, devour these
> things with your punishments, but you cannot
> trample all things under your feet. For the more you
> rage, the more they grow . . . I spread my mantle upon
> the day and night; I do a lot of good works by day
> and anoint the sorrows of the night. Thus no one can
> accuse me either way. I am the most prized of God's
> friends on God's throne; God hides no counsel from
> me. I have a royal dwelling place and all things that
> are from God are mine.[5]

In her development of this figure, Wisdom and Caritas
almost become synonymous. She embodies God's
decision both to create a universe and enter it in human
form. She becomes the divine loving presence that
infuses all creation. Caritas is a truly feminine figure
encompassing the roles of mother, matrix, matter and
womb. The substance of creation is love and within this
the incarnation is prefigured. Caritas is the figure linking
the divine intention with the world's destiny. The purpose of the universe is to incarnate Christ. This starts

with the birth of Jesus but expands through the work of Caritas to involve all humankind.

Caritas is portrayed in the second vision of *The Book of Divine Works* which is depicted as an impressive wheel in the middle of the breast of God. On the wheel are symbols from *Scivias*. There are two circles – one of luminous fire and one of black fire. Other circles are of ether, watery air, and clear air. A thin stratum of air seems to extend over the whole circle and raise up small clouds. In the middle is a human figure with extended arms forming a cross. Four animal heads appear at the four sides – a leopard, a wolf, a lion, and a bear. Their exhalations extend across the figure to form other creatures. Stars and planets also appear. All these figures are connected with the human figure. The figure containing the circle shines with bright light. Hildegard hears a voice saying:

> God has composed the world out of its elements for the glory of God's name. God has strengthened it with the winds, bound and illuminated it with the stars, and filled it with the other creatures . . . The shape of the world exists everlastingly in the knowledge of the true Love which is God: constantly circling, wonderful for human nature, and such that it is not consumed by age and cannot be increased by anything new. It rather remains just as God has created it, everlasting until the end of time.[6]

Here the masculine and feminine elements of God are securely balanced. As already seen in Chapter 3, the circumference represents the fatherhood of God. In its centre the figure of Caritas symbolises the divine motherhood in the various aspects of Wisdom, Christ, Mary, women and humankind in general. She represents the human face of God mothering humanity, the immanent God gently revealing herself to fallen human beings.

In the final vision in *The Book of Divine Works* the figure of Caritas is set in a wheel consisting of four quadrants. The upper left is green which shows that the world is eternally fresh in the mind of God. The red upper right quadrant shows the glory of the cosmos at the end of time. The darkness and pallor at the base of the circle show the anguish of existence in time.

> Now I saw her adorned differently from the way in which she appeared earlier to me. Her countenance shone like the sun, her clothing was a flaming kind of scarlet, and about her neck she had a golden ribbon adorned with costly gems. She wore shoes as radiant as the lightning.
>
> Before the figure's face appeared a tablet that gleamed like crystal. And on it was the following inscription: 'I shall display myself in beauty, shining like silver. For the divinity, who is without beginning, shines forth in great splendour.'[7]

The wheel starts spinning as the ages roll past but the richly adorned woman in the centre representing the Love at the heart of God remains constant. Although the Virtues fade away, justice declines, the greening

Caritas

power of life on earth is reduced in every seed and the pattern of the seasons is disrupted, God's constancy is maintained in Love:

> Love is quietly attached, so to speak, to God's will in that perfection by which God's power overcomes everything . . . This is because everything good takes place out of Love. Her countenance shines like the sun and tells us in this way that we should turn every aim of our hearts towards the true sun.[8]

In vision eight, Caritas interacts with two other Virtues: Humility and Peace. Hildegard sees them as three female figures circling. Caritas speaks of their interaction:

> I am Love, the splendour of the living God. Wisdom has influenced me, and the humility rooted in the living fountain is my helper. Peace is associated with humility. Through the splendour that is my essence, the living light of the blissful angels shines . . . I have designed the human species, which has its roots in me like a shadow, just as one can see the shadow of every object in water. And so I am a living fountain because all creation is like a shadow within myself. As regards this shadow, the human species is formed from fire and water, just as I am both 'fire' and 'living water'. The human species has within its soul the ability to arrange everything according to its own wish.[9]

This is a beautifully refined vision that sets out Hildegard's mature thinking on the role of Caritas in the creation and salvation of the universe. It contains notions of creation existing in the mind of God and then becoming incarnate:

> My splendour has always overshadowed the prophets who in holy inspiration foretold the future, just as everything that God intended to create was only a shadow until it became a reality. But Reason speaks by means of sound, and this sound is, so to speak, a thought and a word and – to a certain degree – a deed (*verbum quasi opus*). Out of this shadow the book *Scivias* emerged. It was composed by a woman who was, so to speak, only a shadow of strength and health because such qualities had no effect in her.[10]

This interrelationship (see Chapter 3) is attributed to the work of Wisdom:

> In this shadow Wisdom distributes everything to the same degree so that nothing can exceed another thing in weight, and so that nothing can be moved by another thing to become what it is not . . . Out of her own being and by herself she has formed all things in love and tenderness.[11]

Queen of the Virtues is Humility. She appears in the Pillar of the Saviour's humanity in a vision in *Scivias* and has a mantle like transparent crystal. On her white hair sits a three-pronged crown with green, red and white jewels. The green ones represent the notion of *viriditas* (see Chapter 10), the fruitful power in the world, here seen as the blossoming of the Virtues. The red and white represent the resurrection and the ascension. On her breast is a mirror in which is reflected the Son of God. But she is more developed in the vision in *The Book of Divine Works* described above. Here she is set against the arrogance of Satan:

> Arrogance is always evil because it oppresses everything, disperses everything, and deprives everything. By way of contrast, humility does not rob people or take anything from them. Rather, it holds together everything in love. God has condescended to the Earth in love and brought together all the powers of the virtues. For the virtues strive toward the Son of God, just as a virgin rejects men and calls Christ her bridegroom. Such virtues are associated with humility when Christ goes with them to the wedding feast of the King.[12]

The third figure in this beautiful vision is Peace:

> Everything God has made has been made in love, humility, and peace. Therefore, we too should be fond of love, we should strive for humility, and we should keep the peace so that we do not perish with those who have scorned these virtues from the moment of their birth.[13]

In *The Book of Life's Merits* she is a strong character, allied to justice:

> Those who utter this evil speech are cast out through me; for I have been appointed always to be glad and rejoice in all good things. For the Lord Jesus abates

and consoles all pain, He who bore pain in His own body.

And, because He is the restorer of justice, I choose to unite myself to Him and sustain Him always, free of hatred and envy and all evils. And I also choose to present a joyful face to Your justice, O God.[14]

Discretion appears regularly as a significant Virtue. It roots Hildegard's visions in the earthiness that characterises a great deal of her writing. It is the gift of the Holy Spirit, who enables people to reflect on their actions and modify them as necessary and is related to the notion of *speculum Dei* (see Chapter 6) which enables us to reform our lives by examining them in the light of reason. It informs much of her counselling as seen in the advice given to the Abbess Hazzecha, who wanted to give up her responsible office to become a hermit:

A person who toils more than her body can bear is rendered useless in her spirit by ill-judged toil and abstinence. Living hopelessly and joylessly, that person's sense often fails. She is fettered by grievous sickness and thus she leaves what she began without discretion, unfinished and in this way, her last condition will be worse than the earlier one.[15]

In *The Book of Life's Merits* Discretion is seen as the fruit of a true contemplation and is set against immoderation. It is related to Compassion and Mercy which are essential to remedy human sickness. Mercy is contrasted with the figure of Hardness of Heart who sends forth only a blank unfeeling stare. Mercy lifts up the broken-hearted and soothes their pain.

Chastity was a central virtue for Hildegard, central to her calling as a monastic virgin and modelled on the chastity of the Virgin Mary. In one vision she is dressed in a tunic more brilliant and pure than crystal shining like water reflecting the sun. In her womb is a pure infant called 'Innocence'. It is associated in her thinking with freedom:

> For I have passed through the pure fountain, Who is the sweet and loving Son of God.[16]

In *The Book of Life's Merits* Chastity is set against the vice Luxury:

> I will surround God's image with filth . . . Why should I restrain myself and why should I tear myself away from the favours of a luxurious life and a saving mind? . . . If I do not do what the flesh demands, I will be angry, sad, deceitful, tormenting, and entangled with unrest. Heaven, therefore, has its own justice and earth seeks its own favours.[17]

Chastity replies:

> I sit in the sun and I look at the King of kings when I perform all my good works freely. I do not want the tail of the scorpion that wounds you with uncleanliness. I have the joy of honesty and modesty in a pleasant life, for the pleasant life that I have does

not restrain me with the blasphemy of baseness nor does it wound me with unclean lewdness.[18]

The Virgin Mary

For Hildegard the Virgin Mary was divine. This is clear from her writing about Wisdom and in her ordering of her songs. It is likely that the manuscript of the songs was put together late in her life, possibly in the last ten years. The oldest manuscript, that to be found in the library of the Dendermonde monastery in Belgium was almost certainly made under Hildegard's supervision as a gift for the monks of Villers. The songs would probably not have been conceived of together, but composed at different times and then ordered into the collection, *The Symphony of the Harmony of Celestial Revelation*. In this the songs of Mary are placed between those to God the Father and the Holy Spirit, in the centre of the Trinity. In a later manuscript, probably put together while she was being considered for sainthood, the Marian songs are placed where Mary belongs in orthodox theology, at the head of the section to the virgins. We have already seen how Hildegard's devotion to Mary may have grown out of the early loss of her mother. This resulted in some of her most beautiful music being directed to the Virgin.

She surrounds Mary with a profusion of imagery, like the rising dawn and the greening branch as in the opening antiphon. She draws on the surrounding nature traditions that can be seen in the face of the green man on the pillars of the monastery of Disibodenberg where she spent much of her youth. This is developed in her hymn

O viridissima virga, in which she likens the Virgin Mary to a greening branch in which the birds build their nests:

> O praise a branch of great greenness, Mary, you answer some of the changing uncertain questions the saints have been asking.
>
> And when the time comes for your branches to produce fragrant blossoms, Mary, may you be worshipped, for the warmth of the sun is distilled in you like the perfume of balsam.
>
> For in you is growing a fair flower, that released fine perfume to all aromatic herbs, which once had been arid. And everyone could see all of this was your greening.
>
> Therefore the skies dropped gentle dew on rolling meadows, and all the earth was filled with laughing joy, since from your innermost being the fields of wheat came springing up and because all the birds of the air have tended nests safely inside you. And from then on there was food for human beings, the pleasure of great feasts and banqueting halls.
>
> Therefore, O lovely virgin, there can be no ending to the joy in you. All of these things were despised by Eve, but today there is praising on high.[19]

Scholars have drawn attention to how the Virgin represents a mixture of elements from the Egyptian goddess Isis, the Greek goddess Demeter, and Aurora, the Roman goddess of the dawn. She draws elements from Caritas, is an incarnation of Wisdom and plays a significant part in the concept of Ecclesia. She is the Bride of God. In Hildegard's vision of Ecclesia, the sunrise of joy resounds with sweetest music for the Virgin Mary. Ecclesia and Mary are linked in singing and dancing by dint of giving birth to the 'Song' of God. Hildegard uses music as an emblem for both Mary and Ecclesia.

Synagogue and Ecclesia

Behind Mary are two other highly significant feminine forms – Synagogue and Ecclesia. Synagogue represents the Jewish tradition from which Ecclesia is born. These two figures are not set against one another, but are seen in continuity with one another. Hildegard's view of the Jewish tradition is that it incarnated God's Wisdom in the shape of the prophets and the patriarchs, who prefigure the coming of Christ.

> After this, I saw the image of a woman, pale from her head to her navel and black from her navel to her feet; her feet were red, and around her feet was a cloud of purest whiteness. She had no eyes, and had put her hands in her armpits; she stood next to the altar that is before the eyes of God, but she did not touch it. And in her heart stood Abraham, and in her breast Moses, and in her womb the rest of the prophets, each displaying his symbols and admiring the beauty of the Church. She was of great size, like the tower of a city, and had on her head a circlet like the dawn. And again I heard the voice from Heaven saying to me: 'On the people of the Old Testament God placed the austerity of the Law in enjoining circumcision on Abraham; which He then turned into sweet Grace when He gave His Son to those who

believed in the truth of the Gospel, and anointed with
the oil of mercy those who had been wounded by the
yoke of the Law.'[20]

Ecclesia, the church, is developed in visions three, four
and five in *Scivias* Book Two. She is a similar maternal
figure containing and protecting the faithful Christians
and connected to the divine. She appears first in a vision
entitled The Church, Bride of Christ and Mother of the
Faithful with four segments which are put together in
her accompanying account:

> After this I saw the image of a woman as large as a
> great city, with a wonderful crown on her head and
> arms from which a splendour hung like sleeves, shin-
> ing from Heaven to earth. Her womb was pierced like
> a net with many openings, with a huge multitude of
> people running in and out . . . I heard a sound of all
> kinds of music singing about her, 'Like the dawn,
> greatly sparkling.'
>
> And that image spreads out its splendour like a
> garment, saying, 'I must conceive and give birth!'
> And at once, like lightning, there hastened to her a
> multitude of angels, making steps and seats within
> her for people, by whom the image was to be
> perfected.
>
> Then I saw black children moving in the air near
> the ground like fishes in water, and they entered the
> womb of the image through the openings that pierced
> it. But she groaned, drawing them upward to her
> head, and they went out by her mouth, while she
> remained untouched. And behold, that serene light

with the figure of a man in it, blazing with a glowing fire, which I had seen in my previous vision, again appeared to me, and stripped the black skin off each of them and threw it away; and it clothed each of them in a pure white garment and opened to them the serene light, saying to them one by one:

'Cast off the old injustice, and put on the new sanctity.'[21]

But Hildegard's vision of the church is very different from that of other theologians of her day, for she is not unsullied by the world. As she gazes at some of her children in this vision she says:

These children of mine will return again to dust. I conceive and bear many who oppress me, their mother, by heretical, schismatic and useless battles, by robberies and murders, by adultery and fornication, and by many such errors. Many of these rise again in true penitence to eternal life, but many fall in false obduracy to eternal death.[22]

The kindness of her maternal role is emphasised and the Virtues figure prominently in the role of Ecclesia. The red glow on her breast is associated with the virginity of Mary which leads on to a description of the celebrations within Ecclesia which includes all kinds of music.

Vision five has a clear relationship to the vision of Synagogue in that the faithful are contained within the larger figure. It develops the notion of the redeemed further:

And I heard the voice from heaven saying 'This is the blossom of the celestial Zion, the mother and flower of roses and lilies of the valley. O blossom, when in your time you are strengthened, you shall bring forth most renowned posterity.'

. . . And around that maiden I saw standing a great crowd of people, brighter than the sun, all wonderfully adorned with gold and gems.[23]

The Rape of the Church

Vision eleven of Book Three of *Scivias* gives a terrifying picture of Ecclesia in the context of the last days and the fall of Anti-Christ. It is a vision in three segments. In the upper left square five differently coloured animals represent the 'five ferocious epochs of temporal rule'. For example, a yellow lion represents unjustified wars. In the right-hand square the glowing Sunrise of Justice, the Son of Man, sits with a harp on his lap signifying the joyful songs of those who are suffering severe torments. The lower part is devoted to the main event of the last days: an assault on Ecclesia.

Satan the true Anti-Christ is born of a prostitute disowned by her parents and learns from her how to create miracles by means of magic practices to attract people to himself. To achieve total domination he must destroy the church. In contradistinction to Christ who marries his Bride, the Anti-Christ attacks her chastity by raping her. The signs will be familiar to people working with those who have suffered sexual assault:

And I saw again the figure of a woman whom I had previously seen in front of the altar that stands before the eyes of God; she stood in the same place, but now I saw her from the waist down. And from her waist to the place that denotes the female, she had various scaly blemishes; and in that latter place was a black monstrous head ... And from this head down to her knees, the figure was white and red as if bruised by many beatings and from her knees to her tendons where they joined her heels, which appeared white, she was covered in blood. And behold! That monstrous head moved from its place with such a great shock that the figure of the woman was shaken through all her limbs.[24]

Ecclesia is portrayed as a composite figure with a horrific mask over the genitals with fiery eyes, asses' ears and a lion's mouth and nostrils. Figures combining human and beast-like features in medieval iconography usually portray evil, particularly the devil who frequently has horns and distorted features. Hildegard's use of such a technique to portray the defilement of the good gives it a remarkable quality. (It is in line with her attitude to the church discussed in Chapter 2.) It is a powerful contemporary symbol for women trying to protect themselves from the predatory male gaze or sexual abuse.

In the end, in the explanation of the vision, the Anti-Christ is defeated, and Ecclesia is vindicated by the Son of Man:

Ecclesia

And lo, the feet of the figure of the woman glow white, shining with a splendour greater than the sun's. This is to say that when the son of perdition is laid prostrate, as was said, and many of those who had erred return to the truth, the bride of my Son, standing on a strong foundation, will manifest purity of faith and the beauty that surpasses all the beauty of the glories of earth.[25]

Hildegard's Authority

Through these visions Hildegard redefines the role of the church. But it is not without its problems. By feminising the church she lays herself open to the dualistic trap of male–female equalling domination–subordination. In this she follows medieval notions of women as the inferior sex. Ecclesia is the bride subject to her divine husband, Christ. She becomes a virgin with the maternal function of giving birth to and protecting human beings through her pure doctrine and her sexual purity. But she turns the image around and uses it to criticise the male clergy and encourage the feminine virtues. Her development of this role links powerfully with Hildegard's own role in God's scheme as an authoritative mouthpiece of this endangered bride of Christ. She writes about why God now utters new mysteries by the mouth of an unlearned person:

But now the Catholic faith wavers among the nations and the Gospel limps among the people; and the mighty books in which the excelling doctors had summoned up knowledge with great care go unread from shameful apathy, and the food of life, which is the divine Scriptures, cools to tepidity. For this reason, I now speak through a person who is not eloquent in the Scriptures or taught by an earthly teacher; I Who Am speak through her of new secrets and mystical truths, heretofore hidden in books, like one who mixes clay and then shapes it to any form he wishes.[26]

She confirms the authority she received in her commissioning vision which challenged the structures of her day. In the male hierarchies of the Middle Ages, God and the church were at the top. Below them were the kings knights, and barons and below them the clergy and religious and then, at the bottom, the ordinary people. Women were considered mentally weak and generally incapable of high-level thinking. Hildegard would have been viewed initially as a person with nothing to say. Only in exceptional cases would women have any say even about their own destiny. The vision of the blinding light accompanied by heat inside her chest and temporary paralysis, which struck her at the age of forty-three gave her the sense that the authority she desired was given to her. In this moment she became confident in her ability to draw from a divine source.

Exercises

1. What do you know of God? How do you envisage the mystery within you? Repeat a phrase like

  Be still and know that I am God

Use it to arrive at a place of not-knowing, a place of emptiness, a place devoid of images but in which you feel comfortable and held.

2. Imagine a huge circle surrounding the world. Feel the love of God flowing through this and holding human beings and the natural world within it. What are the implications of this for the way we organise our lives?

3. Reflect on your own attitude to love, peace and humility. True humility honours God and the presence of the unknowable but is not weak and yielding to whatever untruth is around. It is the opposite of arrogance which claims to know everything. Humility is close to respect and is an attitude of reverence for the unknown. Kneel in reverence before a favourite icon and acknowledge the unknowability of God. Imagine a strong justice-seeking peace. Imagine this force flowing through you.

4. Feel yourself as part of the wider church and feel the Holy Spirit flowing through you and linking people of faith together. Read Hildegard's antiphon about Ecclesia:

  O boundless Ecclesia,
  The divine arms are round your waist;
  You are wearing hyacinths.

You are the perfume from the wounding of the
    nations,
And the city of knowledge.
O, O, again and again you are bathed
In beautiful sound
And shine with sparkling gems.

Feel yourself in the womb of the church and curl up
and feel safe.

6

VISIONS

Antiphon: O virtus Sapientiae

> O the power of Wisdom,
> You in circling, encircle all things.
> You are embracing everything
> In a way that brings life into being:
> For you have three wings.
> One of them reaches highest heaven,
> And another is sweating in earth,
> And the third is flying everywhere.
> Therefore, it is right to give you praise,
> O Sophia Wisdom.[1]

The visionary experiences are central to an understanding of Hildegard's authority and thought. They were her main source of Wisdom. Although difficult to read and sometimes strikingly unusual, the verbal 'text' of the visions presents a powerful way of accessing truth. This valuing is reflected in other aspects of Hildegard's life and work. Her trust in the visionary experience as the main source of her theology shows her clear trust of the intuitive and non-verbal.

> The perception of our inner vision teaches us what is divine.[2]

The visions of Hildegard are central to her theology. Hildegard is able both to trust the intuitive visionary experience and to interpret it in words. Her visions are not a private, inward-looking spirituality but the source of a life focussed on issues of truth and justice. In the Middle Ages there was a greater trust of the visual image as a source of truth. It was after Hildegard, during the Renaissance and particularly after the Enlightenment, that people started to define truth as resting in words and text. From these visual experiences Hildegard drew most of her theology and all of her authority. This is clear from the way in which the pictures are placed in the text. Sometimes they are full-page illustrations while others are L-shaped embracing the text, and others use a tall narrow format that fits the painting into one column of a page. Such a placing would indicate that text and image were conceived as a closely interlinked entity and that the pictures were not just 'illustrations' added later to illuminate the text.

There is a fundamental problem in pursuing this relationship further. The pictures go with two of the texts – *Scivias* and the *The Book of Divine Works*. The problem relates to the loss of the manuscript of Rupertsberg *Scivias* which disappeared from Dresden during World War II. Contemporary work can only be done from black and white photographs of this manuscript and a handmade copy in full colour in the Abtei St Hildegard at Eibingen. This means we do not have any access to Hildegard's original paintings. But even here there is an area of mystery. It is not clear what part Hildegard had in the production of the illuminations. It is likely that they were painted by her nuns under her direction. It is possible that she scratched an outline on her wax tablet (as portrayed in her self-portrait) at the moment of illumination which may mean that in this she was sketching the picture and dictating the text to Volmar at the same time.

Although Hildegard's work is rooted in the traditions of her time, she brings her own unique exuberance to the paintings. The figures often stretch outside the drawn frames that in the work of other artists would have contained them. The unique features include the use of burnished gold and of silver which represents the living light that characterised her visions. It was a risky technique because silver tarnishes. The other colours referred to in the text are blue, green, purple, red, 'subdued colours' and the colour of iron. To these were added soft pinks and beige, orange and ochre. She resisted the regularisation of geometric shapes by the use of compass and ruler which she regarded as a human intervention in the divine nature of the experience. Her use of colour was highly symbolic as we have seen in the vision of the Trinity described in Chapter 3.

The use of perspective is also distinctively her own. *Scivias* contains many architectural forms, and Hildegard had a clear sense of the sacred element in these. Only one is a clear representation. That is the one at the beginning of *Scivias* in which she receives her vision within a building. The others are the many crenelated shapes and tower-like forms in the visions. The shapes are often at an oblique angle with walls sometimes continuing outside the frame, and the human figures in relation to them are sometimes upside down. These features in the visions may reflect the building that would have been going on at the Rupertsberg during the last three years of the work on *Scivias*, or the early experience of building work at the Disbodenberg. They display a concern for regular patterns involving stones laid like walls. All the architectural motifs show a great sense of stability (however angled they might be) and form an important part of the non-figural elements in the visions. For example, the seventh vision of Book Three of *Scivias* portrays the Trinity as the corner of a building.

Of this Hildegard writes:

Thus the Father, the Son and the Holy Spirit testify that they are in no way disunited in power, even though they are distinguished in Persons, because they work together in the unity of the simple and immutable substance.[3]

The general orientation of the visions is sometimes set by winds blowing in on various sides. Sometimes this is done by beasts rather than human figures. But when the orientation is referred to in the text there is no consistent placing of the compass points. The east for example, may be at the top or at the bottom.

Many of the visions include a self-portrait at the foot of the picture. This is sometimes connected to the vision by means of a scroll. Some of these were painted later, possibly in the interests of pressing for her canonisation and emphasising her authority and connection with them. Others appear to have been part of the original design.

The Nature of the Visionary Experiences

The nature of visionary experiences has been the subject of some debate. Hildegard received the first visions at the age of three, and they continued into her old age. During the visions she remained conscious. The still pictures that we have today cannot recapture dramatic moving images which were filled with colour, sound and movement. From the *Life* comes the following account which starts with the way in which Hildegard conceived her visions as relating to issues of justice:

> In the eleven hundredth year after Christ's incarnation, the teaching of the apostles and the burning justice which he had set in Christians and spiritual people began to grow sluggish and irresolute. In that period I was born, and my parents, amid sighs, vowed me to God. And in the third year of my life I saw so great a brightness that my soul trembled; yet because of my infant condition I could express nothing of it. But in my eighth year I was offered to God, given over to a spiritual way of life, and till my fifteenth I saw many things, speaking of a number of them in a simple way, so that those who heard me wondered from where they might have come or from whom they might be.
>
> Then I too grew amazed at myself, that whenever I saw these things deep in my soul I still retained outer sight, and that I heard this said of no other human being. And, as best I could, I concealed the vision I saw in my soul. I was ignorant of much in the outer world, because of the frequent illness that I suffered,

from the time of my mother's milk right up to now: it wore my body out and made my powers fail.

Exhausted by all this, I asked a nurse of mine if she saw anything save external objects. 'Nothing', she answered, for she saw none of those others. Then, seized with great fear, I did not dare reveal it to anyone; yet nonetheless, speaking or composing, I used to make many affirmations about future events, and when I was fully perfumed by this vision I would say many things that were unfathomable (*aliena*) to whose who listened.[4]

She goes on to describe how weeping and blushing were part of the experience and she told only 'a highborn nun', Jutta, who in turn told a monk. The vision in her forty-third year was special:

I was forced by a great pressure (*pressura*) of pains to manifest what I had seen and heard. But I was very much afraid, and blushed to utter what I had so long kept silent. However, at that time my veins and marrow became full of that strength which I had always lacked in my infancy and youth.

I intimated this to a monk who was my *magister* ... Astonished, he bade me write these things down secretly, till he could see what they were and what their source might be. Then, realising that they came from God, he indicated this to his abbot, and from that time on he worked at this [writing down] with me, with great eagerness.

In that same [experience of] vision I understood the writings of the prophets, the Gospels, the works of other holy men, and . . . those of certain philosophers, without any human instruction, and I expounded certain things based on these, though I scarcely had literary understanding, inasmuch as a woman who was not learned had been my teacher. But I also brought forth songs with their melody, in praise of God and the saints, without being taught by anyone, and I sang them too, even though I had never learnt either musical notation or any kind of singing.[5]

It is the quality of living light that pervades all her visions. There is no description of ecstatic experience. What is in the visions is a quality of knowing, of seeing clearly for the first time. In the visions she sees and knows simultaneously.

The Nature of the Visions

Hildegard described the language in which she received her visions as

'an unknown language yet to be heard, not in the ordinary human form of expression'. From this it was dictated to Volmar in a mixture of German and Latin whose task it was to be 'a file, to eagerly smooth this speech so it receives the right sound for human ears'.[6]

It has been suggested by Oliver Sacks, among others, that the visions were a result of migraine, identifying such features as the bright stars as part of the migraine experience. He writes:

Our literal interpretation would be that she experienced a shower of phosphenes in transit across the visual field, their passage being succeeded by a negative scotoma ... Invested with this sense of ecstasy, burning with profound theophorous and philosophical significance, Hildegard's visions were instrumental in directing her towards a life of holiness and mysticism ... One must go to Dostoievski, who experienced on occasion ecstatic epileptic auras to which he attached momentous significance, to find an adequate historical parallel.[7]

However, what is often not mentioned is, as Sacks adds, that this does not invalidate what Hildegard was given as part of the experience. If we believe in a God capable of speaking through human suffering, it is possible that the visions are *both* part of a migraine experience and a manifestation of divine truths.

Exploring the Visions

Hildegard's first book *Scivias* sets out the overarching scheme of God in the world from creation to salvation by means of a series of visions. Each vision is followed by a verbal account of the experience and then pages (sometimes many) of explanation. The striking quality is in the intuitive flash that characterises both the vision and the immediate writing. The other book that contains the visions is *The Book of Divine Works*. In this Hildegard develops the idea of Caritas (see Chapter 5). Hildegard ends each vision in *Scivias* with:

Therefore whoever has knowledge in the Holy Spirit and wings of faith, let this one not ignore My admonition, but taste it, embrace it and receive it in his soul.[8]

The rest of this chapter is devoted to consideration of some of the visions and the exercises at the end invite you to visualise the love of God, as Hildegard did.

Creation and the Fall

This is the second vision of the first book of *Scivias*.

Then I saw as it were a great multitude of very bright living lamps, which received fiery brilliance and acquired an unclouded splendour. And behold! A pit of great breadth and depth appeared, with a mouth like the mouth of a well, emitting fiery smoke with great stench, from which a loathsome cloud spread out and touched a deceitful, vein-shaped form. And, in a region of brightness, it blew upon a white cloud that had come forth from a beautiful human form and contained within itself many and many stars, and so doing, cast out both the white cloud and the human form from that region.[9]

Her explanation of this vision is that those who trust God will shine as fiery lamps reflecting the beauty and glory of God and that they withstand the onslaughts of Lucifer by trusting in the immutability of God. Hell is depicted as a great mouth exuding foul-smelling smoke. Below the falling human figure of Adam is a beautiful garden with fresh flowers and grass and sweet-smelling spices. Paradise underpins the picture. Eve is depicted

The Fall

as a white cloud issuing from Adam's side filled with stars. These represent the whole of the human race. Within Eve is the potential for human redemption.

The World as a Cosmic Egg – The Universe and its Symbolism

This is the third vision of the first book of *Scivias* and perhaps one of the more difficult images to penetrate. It also has a great deal of given text associated with it. It is a vivid text giving a clear impression that the painting is a 'still' version of what was a highly dramatic scene with winds blowing and fire sparkling as all the elements are held in balance:

> After this I saw a vast instrument, round and shadowed, in the shape of an egg, small at the top, large in the middle and narrowed at the bottom. Outside it, surrounding its circumference, there was bright fire with, as it were, a shadowy zone under it. And in that fire there was a globe of sparkling flame so great that the whole instrument was illuminated by it, over which three little torches were arranged in such a way that by their fire they held up the globe lest it fall. And that globe at times raised itself up, so that much fire flew to it and thereby its flames lasted longer; and sometimes sank downward and great cold came to it, so that its flames were more quickly subdued. But from the fire that surrounded the instrument issued a blast with whirlwinds, and from the zone beneath it rushed forth another blast with its own

The Universe

whirlwinds, which diffused themselves hither and thither throughout the instrument.[10]

Hildegard goes on to describe how this zone is filled with winds, thunder, storms, fire and stones. She then turns to the area beneath this zone which is purest ether containing two torches. This time the voice from heaven says:

> The visible and temporal is a manifestation of the invisible and eternal God, Who made all things by His will, created them so that His Name there would be known and glorified, showing in them not just the things that are therefore visible and temporal, but also the things that are invisible and eternal. Which is demonstrated by this vision you are perceiving.[11]

She explains how the egg in the vision is God coming to birth. The fire is there to consume those outside the true faith and warm those within it.

Christ's Sacrifice and the Church

Vision six of Book Two of *Scivias* is a striking vision of the crucifixion. This is not the isolated phenomenon that we associate with later artistic practices. Hildegard never portrays the crucifixion on its own. It is always part of a cosmic scheme.

> And after these things I saw the Son of God hanging on the cross, and the aforementioned image of a woman coming forth like a bright radiance from the

ancient counsel. By divine power she was led to Him, and raised herself upward so that she was sprinkled by the blood from His side; and thus, by the will of the Heavenly Father, she was joined with Him in happy betrothal and nobly dowered with His body and blood.

And I heard the voice from Heaven saying to Him: 'May she, O Son, be your Bride for the restoration of My people; may she be a mother to them, regenerating souls through the salvation of the Spirit and water.'

And as that image grew in strength, I saw an altar, which she frequently approached, and there each time looked devotedly at her dowry and modestly showed it to the Heavenly Father and His angels. Hence when a priest clad in sacred vestments approached that altar to celebrate the divine mysteries, I saw that a great calm light was brought to it from Heaven by angels and shone around the altar until the sacred rite was ended and the priest had withdrawn from it. And when the Gospel of peace had been recited and the offering to be consecrated had been placed upon the altar, and the priest sang the praise of Almighty God, 'Holy, Holy, Holy, Lord God of Hosts,' which began the mystery of the sacred rites, Heaven was suddenly opened and a fiery and inestimable brilliance descended over that offering and irradiated it completely with light, as the sun illumines anything its rays shine through . . .

And when these mysteries were finished, as the priest withdrew from the altar the calm light from Heaven, which, as said, had shone round the whole altar, was drawn up again into the secret places of

Heaven. And again I heard the voice from the supernal heavens, saying to me:

The Church was joined to Christ in His Passion and dowered with His blood.[12]

The Jealousy of God

A striking image, linked to the image of Wisdom found in the antiphon at the beginning of this chapter, forms the fifth vision of the third book of *Scivias*.

After this, I looked, and behold! In the north corner, where the building's two kinds of wall joined, there appeared a head of marvellous form . . . And this head was fiery in colour, sparkling like a fiery flame; and it had a terrible human face, which looked in great anger toward the North. From the neck down I saw nothing to this figure's body, for the rest of it was hidden by its pressing into the corner. But I saw its head, a bare human head. It was not covered by hair like a man's or by a veil like a woman's; but it was more manly than womanly, and very terrible to see.[13]

God's fiery head sees all injustices face to face:

It is not covered by hair like a man's or by a veil like a woman's; for it feels no masculine anxiety about being conquered by one superior in strength, nor has it any feminine weakness as of a timid mind afraid that it cannot conquer its opponents.[14]

Hildegard goes onto interpret this image as the jealousy of God. One wing of the wall is a mirror, *Speculum Dei*, which is very significant in her thinking. This is a quality of self-awareness given by God and linked to the ability to discern good and evil which is related to reason:

> He [God] has so constituted you [human being] that, when you act with wisdom and discretion, you feel Him in your reason . . . These powers flourish where there is reason, for all of them make people know God, so that they may choose what is just.[15]

On the Articulation of the Body

This is the fourth vision of *The Book of Divine Works* and it represents a long theological working out of the relationship of human beings to the cosmos. Hildegard sees the firmament related to the earth. Embers come from the fire in the firmament to the earth which is protected from excessive damage by a layer of ether. A fog also proceeds from it which causes plagues and illnesses. This is opposed by watery air:

> I saw how this moisture from the gentle layer of air flowed over the Earth. This air revived the Earth's greening power and caused all fruits to put forth seeds and become fertile . . . Right in the layer of air I beheld a cloud of pure brightness, which was connected to it and was linked at both ends, so to speak, to the other clouds of the firmament. The cloud's centre was curved like a bow and reached to the above-

On the Articulation of the body

mentioned layer of air ... In the human form God wanted also to relate all these signs to the salvation of the soul.[16]

Hildegard continues to show how the elements relate to one another and that when they are in balance they produce fruitfulness. She links this with human beings:

> Whenever we believers simply go about our work in life, our thoughts are turned in proper longing toward what is useful and fruitful. And so our thinking affects our greening power to bring forth many fruits of holiness.[17]

She revisits the theme of the circle as a metaphor of God's strength. From God's throne, which is divine eternity, fly sparks like the sun's rays from which all radiance emanates. All creatures have a radiance – greenness, seeds, buds and all forms of beauty. She develops the theme of humanity being made in the image of God:

> Like the curvature of a revolving wheel, the top of the human head is the brain against which there leans a ladder with various stages of ascent – the eyes for seeing, the ears for hearing, the nose for smelling, the mouth for speaking ... For God has formed us and enlivened us with the living breath of the soul. The Divinity has provided us with flesh and blood, filled us out and strengthened us with bones, just as earth is strengthened with rock ... The crown of the human head indicates the beginning of the soul's action, which orders and plans all human deeds in accord with prudent reason ... The sphere of the human head indicates the roundness of the firmament, and the right and balanced measurements of our head

reflect the right and balanced measurement of the firmament . . .

God has formed humanity according to the model of the firmament and strengthened human power with the might of the elements. God has firmly adapted the powers of the world to us that we breathe, inhale, and exhale these powers like the sun, which illuminates the earth, sends forth its rays, and draws them back again into itself . . .

The three upper elements are indicated by the human head . . . Within the soul three powers exist: understanding (*comprehensio*) by which the soul grasps heavenly and earthly things through the power of God; insight (*intelligentia*) by which the soul has the greatest insight when it recognises the evil of sin . . . And finally, execution (*motio*) by which the soul moves itself as it accomplishes holy works.[18]

The theme of greening force is developed by seeing the soul as the greening life-force in the flesh. In this frame the Virtues play a crucial part:

Similarly our conscience sends to the soul the moisture of tears when sin grows cold within us and when integrity along with other good deeds, instils into the soul the warmth of heavenly longing. In the same way, the other powers of virtue hasten to assist the strength that pours out the dew of holiness into believers.[19]

Phases of life are paralleled by the seasons:

In the youthful ripening period of life, we come into complete flower. In old age, we are brought back to the period of fading, just as earth in summer is adorned with flowers by its greening power and later transformed by the chill of winter's pallor.

When the soul overcomes the body in such a way that the body is in agreement with the soul in goodwill and simplicity of heart, and refreshed by good treatment as if by nourishing food, we cry out in our longing for heaven: 'How sweet are the words of justice to my throat – even sweeter than honey to my mouth.'[20]

The moon is conceived of as nourisher:

God established the moon to relate to the seasons in such a way that it would give nourishment at all times, as a mother nourishes her child first with milk and later with more substantial food. At its waning the moon becomes weak, and therefore to a certain degree it allows the seasons to be nourished, so to speak, with milk. At its waxing, on the other hand, the moon nourishes the seasons with substantial food.[21]

Human beings are intended to be showered by God's love. Hildegard sees the soul as linked with fire:

The power of the soul clothes us with flesh and blood and completes us as a total unity, just as all the fruits of the Earth are ripened by the blowing of the winds. Through the fiery capacity of the soul, we are also able to realise that we possess God, and through the breath of the Spirit we understand that we can act within our body. On this account, we have received the following principle from God: to do correctly whatever we do . . .

The soul is like the mistress of a house. God has formed the whole abode for the soul's sake so that it can take possession of that house.[22]

This carefully worked theology of human beings in relation to the earth ends with a powerful statement from God, which is an exegesis of the opening of John's Gospel:

I who am without origin and from whom every beginning goes forth, I who am the Ancient of Days, do declare that I am the day by myself alone. I am the day that does not shine by the sun; rather by me the sun is ignited. I am the reason that is not made perceptible by anyone else; rather, I am the One by whom every reasonable being draws breath. And so to gaze at my countenance I have created mirrors in which I consider all the wonders of my originality, which will never cease. I have prepared for myself these mirror forms so that they may resonate in a song of praise . . .

Humanity is the guise in which my Son, clothed in heavenly power, reveals himself as the God of all creation and as the Life of life . . . Blessed, therefore, are those who abide in God![23]

Exercises

1. Self abandonment to divine providence. Imagine yourself in God's arms or upheld by a ring of angels. Let yourself go and allow them to take you where they will. When you end the visualisation see if there is an indication of a particular step you should take, or a situation you should leave, or one that you should enter.

2. (a) Look at the illustration, The Universe, p. 93. Imagine yourself in the midst of a storm but contained in a small capsule. Feel how the elements of the storm are held in balance within a structure that is a manifestation of God's stability. If you lose the sense of stability look again at the picture and see how the winds, for example, hold the whole picture in balance. Then return to your own image.

(b) Take an egg and meditate on its promise of hope. Imagine it as your own potential within God. Imagine the warmth of God in your heart encouraging your own growth. What are you being called to do?

3. Imagine yourself looking in a mirror held by God. What do you see? Look at your physical body, your spiritual and psychological make-up. See God as accepting it as it is and then ask what changes you are asked to make.

4. (a) Look at the illustration on p. 98. Take a photograph of yourself and set it within a circle. Set

features of the natural world in the circle and draw connections with yourself. Use your drawing as a mandala to guide your meditation.

(b) The vision is an intuitive way of knowing. More people have visions today than are prepared to talk about them. Trust your own visions. Test them. Understand them. Translate them into action.

7

HEALING

Antiphon: O quam mirabilis

1. O how amazing is the fine divine
      blueprint
   That exists in God's heart.
   For in this is all creation planned.
   For when God looked longingly
   At the shape of humankind,
   Divinely formed,
   There every created thing
   Could now be seen inside humankind
   Completely integrated.

2. O how miraculous is
   This inspiration
   Which in this way
   Gave humankind life.[1]

The last vision described in the previous chapter shows why some would regard Hildegard as the first German scientist and medical doctor. She was one of the first to write in depth of the properties of herbs and elements, of the physiology of the human body and how remedies might connect the two together. She spoke openly and clearly of sexuality and of the physical and emotional differences between men and women. Her medical books were well regarded in her time. Joseph Trithemius

(1462–1516) commented on the subtlety of her medical writings which he said could only have been written by a woman. The medical knowledge of his age was the carefully guarded domain of the university educated, the publicly licensed male physicians and the medical guilds.

In Hildegard's day the Rule of Benedict required monasteries to have an infirmary for the care of sick members of the community. The infirmary would also have provided care for the poorer members of the local community who could not afford the services of a physician. In her *Explanation of the Rule of Benedict* Hildegard advocates relaxing dietary restrictions of the convent, allowing the sick to eat the flesh of quadrupeds (such as cattle, sheep or swine) and allowing the elderly and the children to eat more frequently. The Rupertsberg infirmary would have been equipped with beds, medicinal baths, a cupboard for the storage of expensive medicines, a fire for the preparation of special food, mortars and pestles, bandages, lancets for bloodletting, books for the building up of the spiritual life and would perhaps have had its own chapel.

Hildegard was writing at a time when the second Lateran council (1139) forbade monks from pursuing medical studies or practising medicine for profit. The monasteries played an important part in the preservation of medical writings, and the period saw an upsurge in the number of medical texts produced. There was a new emphasis on identifying causes rather than simply providing practical remedies. Hildegard believed that all illnesses were curable except asthma and migraine, which may have been because she suffered from these illnesses herself. She also taught that the four principles of good health were rest (freedom from stress), a balanced diet, exercise and a moral life. And yet all her healing was dependent in God:

> The medicaments given below were prescribed by God to be used against the above named ailments. Either they will heal the person or he will die if God does not will that he be healed.[2]

The Sources

Hildegard's medical works are *Causae et Curae* and *Physica*. *Causae et Curae* starts with God creating the universe and then in Book 2 deals with the causes of disease, human sexuality, psychology and physiology. Books 3 and 4 deal with remedies, Book 5 with prognostics. Book 6 consists of a lunar horoscope. The intention of these texts was arguably different from that of the visionary writings which had inspirational and edifying aspirations. The inconsistencies in the medical writings possibly reflect Hildegard's freedom to change her opinions and ideas in relation to her own observation of the natural world and its relationship to human disease.

The nine books of her *Physica* list the medicinal qualities and uses of plants, elements, trees, stones, fish, birds, quadrupeds, reptiles and metals, and are based on her careful and scientific observation.

Hildegard was probably the first nun to write about medicine and hers is the first documented community to own medical literature. Her writing is quite distinctive. Not only are theology and physiology intertwined in the organisation of the books as a whole but also within the writing itself. The style is highly imaginative, using metaphors that often make it feel more like poetry than medical writing.

In her works she merges two types of medical literature – the books of practical remedies and the large encyclopaedic overviews of human health. This makes her writings innovative and challenging. Although she draws on contemporary literature, she reworks it and reorganises it in accordance with the overarching scheme which she developed more deeply in the cosmology of *The Book of Divine Works*.

In her vision On Human Nature in *The Book of Divine Works* Hildegard sees a human figure set in the firmament and the winds setting the firmament in motion by their gusts. She sees the days getting longer and then shorter. The circle is surrounded by fire. She sees how the winds and the air affect the humours in the human being. Sometimes this results in strength and sometimes in weakening. She likens the humours to a lion that sometimes roars and sometimes is calm. There is a lengthy description of the effects this will have on such organs as the liver, gall bladder and kidneys as well as on the legs. These are also linked with fits of melancholy. The voice says to her:

God has directed for humanity's benefit all of creation which God has formed both on the heights and in the depths. If we abuse our position to commit evil deeds, God's judgement will permit other creatures to punish us. And just as creatures have to serve our bodily needs, it is also easily understood that they are intended for the welfare of our souls.[3]

The Humours

Hildegard's medicine was set in the context of the system of humours that characterised the medieval medical frame. The system had its roots in China and India but was systematised by Hippocrates who was born in 460 BC. In this system the body contained four liquids or humours: blood, phlegm, yellow bile and black bile. When these are in balance the body is healthy and an imbalance causes ill health. The Hippocratic system was revived and elaborated by Galen (AD 130–200) and spread throughout Europe and (translated into Arabic) to the Islamic world. However, the writers of Hildegard's day preferred to return to the more approachable writings of Hippocrates rather than the more complex and verbose texts of Galen. Their system was based on a balance between sensations – hot, cold, wet and dry. This balance could be affected by diet and environment including the season of the year. Disease was conceived of as imbalance:

> Should the above-mentioned humours maintain their correct balance and proper proportion in a person . . . he finds himself in a condition of peace and health. However, when they conflict with each other, the humours make him weak and sick.[4]

The patient could be brought back to health by restoring the balance of the humours. Excesses were removed by bleeding, purging, vomiting or starvation, while deficiency was treated by special diets and medicines. The system also included a theory of personality types,

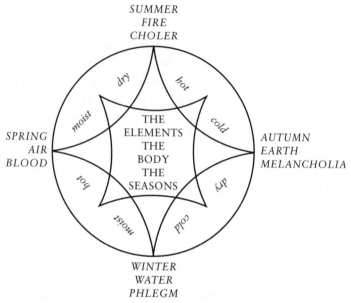

SUMMER
FIRE
CHOLER

dry   hot

moist   cold

THE
ELEMENTS
THE
BODY
THE
SEASONS

SPRING
AIR
BLOOD

AUTUMN
EARTH
MELANCHOLIA

hot   dry

moist   cold

WINTER
WATER
PHLEGM

based on the predominance of one of the humours in the person. The four types were sanguine (excess blood), phlegmatic (excess phlegm), choleric (excess yellow bile) and melancholic (excess black bile). Hildegard wrote in detail of the various personality types. These are the descriptions of them in women:

> *The Sanguine*: Some women are inclined to plumpness, and have soft and delectable flesh and slender veins, and well-constituted blood free of impurities . . . And these have a clear and light colouring, and in love's embraces are themselves lovable; they are subtle in arts, and show self-restraint in their disposition. At menstruation they suffer only a moderate loss of blood, and their womb is well developed for

childbearing, so they are fertile and can take in the man's seed. Yet they do not bear many children, and if they are without husbands, they are well.

The Phlegmatic: There are other women whose flesh does not develop as much, because they have thick veins and healthy, whitish blood (though it does contain a little impurity, which is the source of its light colour). They have severe features, and are darkish in colouring; they are vigorous and practical, and have a somewhat mannish disposition. At menstruation their menstrual blood flows neither too little nor too abundantly . . . And because they have thick veins they are very fertile and conceive easily, for their womb and all their inner organs, too, are well developed. They attract men and make men pursue them, and so men love them well . . . And because they are to some extent mannish on account of vital force [*viriditas*, lit. 'greenness'] within them, a little down sometimes grows on their chin . . .

The Choleric: There are other women who have slender flesh but big bones, moderately sized veins and dense red blood. They are pallid in colouring, prudent and benevolent, and men show them reverence and are afraid of them. They suffer much loss of blood in menstruation; their womb is well developed and they are fertile . . .

The Melancholic: But there are other women who have gaunt flesh and thick veins and moderately sized bones; their blood is more lead-coloured than sanguine, and their colouring is as it were blended with grey and black. They are changeable and free-roaming in their thoughts, and wearisomely wasted away in affliction; they also have little power of resistance, so that at times they are worn out by melancholy. They suffer much loss of blood in menstruation, and they are sterile, because they have a weak and fragile womb.[5]

In her letters she used the concept of personality types based on the humours as the basis for all counselling. In a letter to an abbot she wrote:

Even as man consists of elements, and the elements are conjoined, and none is of any avail to itself without another, so too the modes of behaviour of men are unequal, even though they arise from one and the same breath of life.

There are four modes of behaviour among men: some are hard, some airy, some stormy, some fiery.

One who has the hard mode is sharp in everything ... And as for one who has the airy mode, his mind is always wavering ...

Those who have the stormy mode are not wise, but compound all they do with foolishness; they are not improved by words of wisdom, but shudder at them indignantly.

And those who have the fiery mode aspire to everything worldly and alienate themselves from spiritual people; they shun peace and, wherever they see it, strike at it with some worldly ambition ...

But God gathers to himself some of all those who have such modes of behaviour – when, growing aware, they turn what goes against their souls' salvation back towards God: those who at last fear him, as happened in the case of Saul and many others.[6]

So we can see that the system of humours (unlike the contemporary concept of personality typing) ran through physiology as well as psychology. It tempered the tight links of cause and effect. What works for a choleric man will function very differently in a choleric woman or a sanguine man. It is worth reflecting on this in the context of the fixed procedures and practices of contemporary medicine. Theologically it allows for diversity within a system united by a first principle who is God. Hildegard's diagnoses all start with the humours but these are also conceived in a theological frame:

Their flesh is ulcerated and permeable [to disease]. These sores and openings create a certain storm and smoky moisture in men, from which the *flegmata* arise and coagulate, which then introduce diverse infirmities to the human body. All this arose from the first evil, which man began at the start, because if Adam had remained in paradise, he would have had the sweetest health, and the best dwelling-place, just as the strongest balsam emits the best odour.[7]

Although operating within the frame of her time, especially in the area of diagnoses and prescribed remedies, Hildegard put her own distinctive stamp on the ideas. Her attitude to the place of women in the humourial system varied from the norm. Men at that time were generally regarded as participating more fully in the warmer elements (fire and air) and women in the colder (water and earth). This was an elaboration of Aristotle's notion of the male as active and the female as passive. Although Hildegard wrote of women as a 'weak and fragile and a vessel for man' who therefore needs less exercise and should spend more time sitting than walking or standing, she rejected Aristotle's frame which could be regarded as a cosmic projection of the missionary position. In her view man was associated with earth, because Adam had been created from the dust of the ground. She described woman as having a more airy temperament, and used this to explain greater openness to the intuitive stirrings of the spirit and the subtle changes in her physical environment.

Healing and the Natural World

Herbal remedies were all linked into the system:

> Fennel has a mild heat, and its nature is neither dry nor cold. Eaten raw, it will not harm a person. And however it is eaten it makes people glad, giving them a mild glow, and a pleasant smell, and makes for good digestion. Its seeds are also hot by nature and good for a person's health if it is added to other plants in medicine. For whoever eats fennel or its seeds daily on an empty stomach will lessen the bad and putrid humours and eliminate bad breath and make the eyes see clearly. [*Physica*, Plants, 66][8]

Fennel plays an important part in many of Hildegard's remedies, like this one for insomnia:

If a person is busied with certain problems and cannot sleep, if it is summer, let them take fennel and twice as much yarrow, cook them in a little water, and having removed the water, let them put the herbs on the temples and forehead and tie a cloth over it. And take green sage and sprinkle it with a little wine and put it over the heart and around the neck and they will be rewarded with sleep.

But if it is winter take some fennel seed and yarrow root, cook them in water and place them around the temples and head as said before, and place powdered sage moistened with a little wine over the heart and around the neck, tied down with a cloth over the top, as described, and they will have better sleep. For the heat of the fennel induces sleep, and the heat of the yarrow makes it sound, and the heat of the sage slows the heart and dilates the veins in the neck, so that sleep may come.[9]

Hildegard's writings are underpinned by the medieval concept of 'interrelated fours' – the four elements (air, fire, earth and water), the four seasons, the four humours, the four zones of the earth and the four winds. Each of the elements has particular properties:

Water possesses fifteen powers. They include warmth, air, moisture, flooding, rapidity, and motion. Water gives sap to the trees, taste to the fruit, their greenness to the plants; everything is full of its moisture. It carries the birds, nourishes the fish, allows animals to live in its warmth, returns reptiles to its waves, and keeps everything alive like the Ten Commandments and the Five Books of Moses of the Old Testament that God intended for spiritual knowledge.[10]

She locates the elements in the human body, for example the blood:

> Water is contained in human beings because they have blood. Blood maintains moisture in humans so that the life power in them remains fresh and their bones stay hard.[11]

So the four elements link the natural world with the human body. We are in a reciprocal relationship with the world as the opening antiphon shows:

> Now as mentioned above, in the same way that the elements comprise the world, so too are they the fabric of the human body. And they are diffused and active throughout the body so that the body is held together, and at the same time they are spread throughout the world and work upon it. For, fire, air, water, and earth are in human beings, and humans are made from them.
>
> Thus from fire they derive heat; from air, breath; from water, blood; and from earth, flesh. Moreover, their sight comes from fire; their hearing from air; their movement from water; and their measured tread from earth. And the world prospers when the elements fulfil their roles in a well-ordered fashion, so that heat, dew, and rain, one by one and in moderation, apportion themselves in due season and come to regulate the earth, bringing fruitful and abundant produce

and health. But if they were to fall on the earth suddenly, all at once and unseasonably, the earth would cleave asunder and its produce and health would be ruined.

Likewise, when the elements are properly at work in the body they preserve it and confer health; but when they are at odds in it they waken and kill it.[12]

She believed in the influence of sun and moon on human health.

A person's blood and humours are affected by the time of the moon's movement; specifically, the air moves to good or bad weather following the moon, and, corresponding to them, the blood and humours flow within a person, and the water conservation affects human behaviour.[13]

Women's Health

Hildegard was one of the few writers who saw fit to write on women's health including reproduction. Most of the medieval writers did not differentiate between men and women, only referring to women directly in connection with pregnancy and childbirth. The majority of medieval physicians would not accept women as patients feeling that

they should concentrate their efforts on the worthy sex.[14]

She writes about problems with menstruation, pregnancy and childbirth, barrenness and the problem of unrequited love (distinguishing between men and women). She describes a potion that women can use for unwanted lovers. Herbal baths and gemstones are advised for menstrual pain and there are incantations for infertility. These are written about with real understanding and sensitivity. Here is an example of her advice, quite clearly based on practical experience:

> *For a Difficult Birth.* If a pregnant woman is experiencing many pains while giving birth, one should prudently and with great caution boil some mild plants, specifically fennel and hazel root, squeeze out the water, and then lay them, still hot, on the thigh and the back of the woman, wrap cloths around them and fasten the whole thing so that the pain diminishes and the blocked birth passage may open smoothly and easily. For the harmful cold humours that are present in the woman sometimes make it contract during her pregnancy and close up.[15]

Yet Hildegard follows Augustine in her negative attitude to sexuality and concupiscence, in keeping with her own virginity. In this passage from *Scivias* she suggests that women's nature is to resist man's desire. She distinguishes between male and female desire.

> *Woman's Desire.* One can compare woman's desire with the sun which softens the earth with its warmth and penetrates her, fixed continually so that it brings forth fruit . . . So the female's desire has a soft, gentle,

but still continual warmth in order to conceive and bear offspring.

Man's Desire. When the storm of passion breaks out in a man, it whirs about in him like a mill wheel. For his loins may be compared with a forge into which the arrow dispatches its fire.[16]

She includes medical tips on abortion, birth control or feigning virginity. Her thinking on sexuality builds on a notion of moral freedom and a holistic approach to the union of soul and body, which she struggles to reconcile. Despite the apparently holistic concepts underpinning her own version of the humourial medical system, she sees the soul working out its salvation by divorcing itself from bodily desire. She is not concerned to return to the seemingly perfect ideal sexuality of the Garden of Eden. The new beginning that she is seeking will come from transcending sexuality altogether. It is within this frame that her own vow of chastity fits, and it is interesting to reinterpret this pursuit of virginity by relating it to the contemporary concept of being one's own person.

Viriditas

Central to Hildegard's system is the concept of *viriditas*, life energy or vitality (see Chapter 10). This is central to the immune system. She saw laughing, crying, singing and dancing as linked with the health of the body. Diet was her main way of strengthening this central energy within us. It was inextricably linked with the notion of humours and she recommends a different diet for winter and cold periods. Central to her diet was the cereal grain, spelt, which contains the life energy that enables the cells of the body to be rejuvenated:

> Spelt is the best of grains. It is hot, rich, and full of goodness. It is sweeter than other grains. Eating it promotes sound flesh and healthy blood as well as a happy mind and joyful outlook. And however it is eaten, whether in bread or other food, it is good and pleasant. [*Physica*, Plants, 5][17]

It is easily digestible whether you take it in bread or other forms. Current research has analysed spelt and found that it contains all essential nutrients including carbohydrates, vitamins, a great variety of minerals, dietary fibre, high value proteins in the form of essential amino acids and the fatty acids (lipids) required by the nervous system.

Hildegard's diet was simple, consisting of the grains – spelt, oats, wheat, rye and barley; vegetables – beans, fennel, celery, chickpeas, pumpkin, watercress, beetroot, lettuce, chestnuts, onions, sweetcorn, broccoli; fruits – apples, cherries, quince, black and red currants, grapes, raspberries, blackberries, citrus fruits, melons, dates; fish – pike, perch, roach, grayling, with salmon, herring, caro and trout for the healthy only; meats – poultry, lamb, goat and venison. A number of spices are recommended. For drinking there is water (spring and well rather than mineral), fennel (highly recommended), rosehip and lemon balm tea, spelt coffee and beer (especially for the underweight). She recommends wine but only mixed with water:

Wine is both the blood of the earth and is in the earth as blood is in human beings. It has a certain commonality with human blood and for that reason, like a water wheel, funnels its warmth directly out of the bladder into the marrow and sets it into an extremely burning heat so that the marrow then bestows upon the blood a hot striving of desire. For that reason, a person who wants to drink some strong, noble wine should mix it with water.[18]

Quenched wine is recommended as a treatment for anger and melancholy:

If a person is overcome by anger or melancholy, he should quickly heat some wine on the fire, mix it with cold water, and drink it. In this fashion the vapours from his bile, which has led him into anger, will be suppressed.[19]

Digestion was very important in the maintenance of health.

When a man eats, the fine vessels that are sensitive to taste, distribute the taste throughout the body. The inner vessels – that is, those of the liver, heart and lungs – take the more delicate humour of the food away from the stomach and distribute it throughout the whole body. In this way the person's blood is increased and the body nourished. It is like the way a fire flares up through a blast from the bellows, and the grass turns green and grows because of the wind and the dew. Just as the bellows blow the fire into a flame and the wind and the dew bring forth the grass, so also the humours from food and drink cause the blood, the humour, and a person's flesh to grow and increase.[20]

She sets out recipes to aid digestion:

For Digestive Problems. If a person cannot digest the food he has eaten, he should take the juice from the Easter lily in weight equal to two coins, the juice from burnt saxifrage to the weight of one coin, the juice from a quickly working laxative to the weight of one obolus, ginger to the weight of one obolus, and then a little fine wheat flour. With these juices, he should make a small cake the size of a coin, but a bit thicker, and bake it in the sun or in an oven that has almost cooled down. A person who suffers from the above-mentioned digestive problems should eat this small cake on an empty stomach in the morning when he is warm inside and the food in him is exhausted . . . He should do this until he again feels free in his stomach. For the heat of the Easter lily which is some-what sharp and strong, if it is moderated by the cold of the burnt saxifrage, brings a person's harmful humours into motion; the heat of the ginger releases them; the cold of the quick-working laxative leads them quickly away; and the fine wheat flour streng-thens the stomach so that they do not damage it.[21]

Regular fasting was an important part of her regime. The fast was not total and involved the use of vegetable soup. Hildegard cautioned against extremes.

Spirituality and Health

In Hildegard's writing the notion of spirituality is inextricably intertwined with the physical.

> *The Infusion of the Soul.* What is sent into the body as a soul is breath. Breath is sent from God and receives its reward on the basis of its physical deeds, according to whether they are good or bad. These deeds bind all moral development together. Just as a small child knows nothing at first of what he will later understand because he receives, with growing maturity, the insight into everything, and just as he later grows weary as a result of age, so the soul develops within him and makes progress by means of his works. The soul is wrapped around by good works as with a king's mantle, but it becomes darkened by evil deeds as the earth also is penetrated by water. As waters flow over certain places, so the soul penetrates the body and is more noble than it. Even when our external eyes are closed, the soul often sees the future by means of its prophetic powers because it already knows that it can live without the body.[22]

Her description of the inflowing of the soul in the foetus would grace any contemporary debate of biogenetics. It contains in the middle the beautiful image of the caterpillar that spins silk:

> Then, as God wills it and as he arranged it, the breath of God comes which enlivens this form. Without the mother knowing it, the breath of life comes like a

strong warm wind, like a wind that blows loudly against a wall and streams and fastens itself to every joint and limb of this shape. In this way, the various limbs of this form are gently separated from one another, just as the flowers unfold themselves in the warmth of the sun. But there is still such weakness in this form that it cannot move itself, but only lies there, sleeps, and barely breathes. The spirit of life penetrates the entire form, fills and strengthens it in its marrow and in its veins so that they grow more than before, until the bones are spread out over the marrow and the veins become so strong that they can contain the blood. Now the child begins to move, and the mother feels it as though she received a sudden kick; from then on it remains continually in motion. For the living wind, that is the soul, enters into this form, as was mentioned above, according to the will of almighty God, strengthens it, makes it capable of life, and wanders around within it like a caterpillar that spins silk from which it becomes covered and closed in as with a house. In this form, the spirit of life discerns where the soul can divide itself, bend, and turn about; it also pays attention to all the places where there are veins, dries them out like the inner walls of a reed, and joins itself with the flesh so that by the heat of its fire it becomes red like the blood because the soul is fire. Thus it penetrates the entire form of the child with its breath, just as an entire house will be illuminated by a fire at its centre.[23]

She links brain and soul together through the faculty of reason.

The soul lives in the heart as in a house; causes thoughts to enter and leave as through a door; views them as through a window; and guides their force to the brain as smoke is drawn from a lit fire to a chimney, there to test and judge them . . . Thoughts are the foundation of the knowledge of good and evil, and they arrange all things. Man calls that 'thinking'. Thoughts ground goodness, wisdom, stupidity, and other such things . . . The powers of thought climb to the brain, and the brain holds them fast because the brain provides the moisture for the entire body, just as the dew covers everything. However, if evil noxious humours develop in a person, they send a kind of noxious vapour to the brain.[24]

Spirit Possession

Hildegard believed in the presence of demons as witnessed by her exorcism of the young woman Sigewize who was being treated at another monastery. Hildegard used the intuitive arts in healing by sending a ritual/drama to be carried out. This involved seven priests of good repute wearing priestly vestments and stoles, but unfortunately appears to have been unsuccessful. Sigewize came to Hildegard's convent, and eventually Hildegard succeeded where others had failed by attempting the exorcism during the Triduum, the three-day liturgy of Easter. This shows how she used liturgy within her concept of health. Sigewize would undoubtedly have received counselling and other dietary treatments in support of this spiritual exercise. The contemporary church has much to learn on the use of liturgy in combination with physical and psychological treatments.

The Eyes

Hildegard called the eyes the windows of the soul and they were very important in her diagnoses.

> If a person is sound of body, if he has clear, bright, diaphanous eyes, regardless of the colour, he has the marks of life. If his eyes are as bright and transparent as a white cloud through which another bluish cloud can occasionally be caught sight of, he will live and not die soon ... A person's eyes are indeed the windows of the soul.[25]

Precious Stones and Metals

Hildegard used precious stones and metals freely in her remedies, recommending holding them in the mouth or placing them in liquids to be drunk. Emerald is potentially very valuable because:

> The emerald is formed early in the morning, at sunrise, when the sun is positioned powerfully in its circle ready for its journey. Then the fresh greenness of the earth and crops is at its strongest, since the air is still cold and the sun already hot; and then the plants suck up the garden green freshness like a lamb sucking milk ...
>
> And so the emerald is strongest against all human debility and weakness, since the sun conditions it and all its matter is from the fresh greenness of the air. So let whoever has a pain in the heart or stomach or side have an emerald with them so they can warm the

flesh of their body with it, and they will be better. But if those diseases overwhelm them so that they cannot escape their storm, then let the person place an emerald in the mouth and wet it with saliva, and thus as the saliva is made warm by the stone repeatedly being put in and taken out, the recurrent waves of the illness will surely cease.

And if anyone suffers from epilepsy and falls to the ground, place the emerald in their mouth and their spirit will revive, and after they get up and take the stone from their mouth let them look at it carefully and say: 'Just as the spirit of the Lord filled the globe of the earth, so let it fill the home of my body by His grace so that it can never be moved,' and let them do this for nine consecutive days in the morning, and they will be cured. [*Physica*, Stones, 1][26]

She also saw gold as a powerful remedy:

Gold is hot, and its nature is partly like the sun and partly like the air. Let anyone who is paralysed take gold and heat it so there are no impurities in it and beat it to a powder and take a little flour – about a handful – and knead it with water and add about an obolus of gold powder to this. Let this be eaten fasting in the morning . . .

And again take pure gold and place it in a pot or jug, and when it is heated put it in pure wine so that it is warmed by it, and let the patient drink it warm. And let it be done often, and the illness will depart. [*Physica*, Metals, 1][27]

Animals

Animal are integrated into the systems of the humours and have healing properties.

> The dog is very hot and has a natural affinity for the ways of people, and so he knows and understands them and loves them, and willingly lives with them and is faithful . . .
>
> And if there is a thief in the house, or anyone who has the intention of stealing, the dog will snarl and growl at him and behave differently toward him than to others and follow after him and sniff at him with his nose, and in his way the thief will be known. And he senses a little beforehand those deeds and events, happy or sad, that are going to happen, and gives voice according to his understanding and indicates them: when they are going to be happy he wags his tail gladly: when they are going to be sad he howls mournfully.
>
> The heat that is in a dog's tongue confers health on wounds and ulcers, if he touches it with this heat. [*Physica*, Animals, 20][28]

Exercises

1. Do you have a picture of what sort of person you are? Have you done a course on the Myers-Briggs personality indicators? Can you link these with the

elements? Are you fiery or earthy or watery or airy? Prayerfully look at yourself and imagine how you might adjust your surroundings to accommodate this. Do this honestly and tenderly. After the meditation make the changes in your lifestyle that you have thought about.

2. Imagine the element you most enjoy. Take yourself somewhere where you can experience it, like wind on the top of a hill. Feel the characteristic of the element. What is it that attracts you to it? Feel that characteristic in yourself. It is God-given. Value that characteristic and feel it grow as you are in contact with the element. Come back and draw a picture of yourself connected to the elements of the world.

3. Eat a meal in silence and prayerfully imagining the food circulating within your body and nourishing all the organs.

4. Look into your own eyes. These are the windows of your soul. Look at them and see the beauty in your own soul. Close your eyes and imagine the light of God glowing in your soul. Look again and focus on the beauty of your body.

8

THE MUSIC

Antiphon: Laus Trinitatis

Praise the Trinity
Our life-giving music.
She is creating all things.
Life itself is giving birth.
And she is an angel chorus praising
And the splendour of arcane mysteries,
Which are too difficult to understand.
Also from her true life springs for all. [1]

We have seen in the previous chapter how balance was
central to Hildegard's view of the cosmos. As this antiphon indicates, for Hildegard music was crucial in this
process and therefore central to her theology. Before
reading this chapter I suggest you listen to a recording
of the music. In her day, music was a higher order subject being included in the Quadrivium with astronomy,
geometry and mathematics. However, the study of the
Quadrivium was available only to aristocratic boys,
because women were not considered capable of abstract
thinking. Hildegard, therefore, would not have had
access to this. Her musical education consisted of being
immersed in liturgical music from an early age. It is
unlikely that she wrote down her own music and it is
possible that Volmar was not musically literate. Musical
scribes in the Middle Ages charged a high price for their

services to cover their specialist skill and the cost of the materials for the manuscript. It is possible that a wealthy patron paid for Hildegard's pieces to be written down towards the end of her life.

She stresses the intuitive nature of her processes and her lack of instruction in music and neumes (the notation system of her day) in her *Life*. What she would have had was a total immersion in daily choral singing in the Benedictine tradition, and therefore can be seen as part of an ancient oral tradition. The material would have been held in the memory of the people at the convent. The ability to memorise exists in inverse ratio to the ability to read. In an age where literacy is limited, the memory is correspondingly more retentive. Anyone who has listened to the song repertoire of a class of five-year-olds with limited reading skills will have experienced this. Some material may therefore have been lost, as were later women's songs like those of the beguine Mechtild of Hackeborn, the so-called Flemish nightingale.

Hildegard is nonetheless one of the earliest women composers in Europe whose works have been preserved. She was preceded by Hrotswitha, a tenth-century German Benedictine nun from Candersheim who wrote poetry, drama and music; and Kassia, a Byzantine nun of the early ninth century who wrote about forty-nine liturgical compositions. It is, however, unlikely that Hildegard would have been aware of these women. It is not by accident that the main stream of women composers runs through the convents. These all-female communities gave women a freedom from the round of childbearing and an authority unavailable anywhere else in medieval society. In her Alleluia, Hildegard prays that her own closed up womb will give birth like that of the Virgin Mary. It was in the seventy-seven hymns and *The Play of the Powers* that this wish was most clearly realised. These compositions would not have been possible other than in the context of her chosen monastic vocation.

Music in a Monastic Context

It is impossible to understand Hildegard's music without locating it within its liturgical context. All her pieces were intended for liturgical use and even *Ordo Virtutum*, the morality play with music, may have been associated with the office, being placed at the end of Matins or Vespers. The placing in the liturgical year is, however, not always clear as particular days or Offices are seldom specified. They all use forms like antiphons, hymns and responsories that would have been part of the regular Offices or the celebration of the Mass. Hymns would have been sung by the whole congregation. The antiphons and responsories may have been sung by a small group or a soloist. The antiphons were associated with the psalms, while the responsories have a special role in the main Offices especially Matins (see Chapter 4).

In the Middle Ages it was quite common to add to the bank of available liturgical material especially for the celebration of particular local saints. Hildegard's antiphons for St Rupert and St Disibod are in this tradition. It was also not uncommon to revisit traditional themes as Hildegard did, particularly in the pieces concerning the Virgin Mary and the Holy Spirit. Her works include one Alleluia, one Kyrie and seven sequences for use with the Mass. For the Office she wrote forty-three anitphons for use with psalms (see below), eighteen responsories, three hymns and four devotional songs.

Her collection of songs is entitled *Symphonia armonie celestium revelationum* (*The Symphony of the Harmony of Heavenly Revelations*). It is likely that the *Symphony* was not conceived as a grand cycle but was an ordering by Hildegard (in the case of the Dendermonde manuscript) of diverse material created on different occasions. From the addition of the psalm tones in the margins of one of the manuscripts, it looks as though some of the songs may have had an independent life before being linked (somewhat uneasily) with the psalm tones.

The Choirs of Angels

The sixth vision of *Scivias* is one of the most magnificent of the visions and impressive in its execution as a painting. It is an amazing picture of the armies of angels centring upon the mystery of God. All these ranks of angels are:

> singing with marvellous voices all kinds of music about the wonders that God works in blessed souls, and by this God was magnificently glorified. And I hear the voice from Heaven, saying to Me:

> God wonderfully formed and ordered His creation.[2]

Her explanation of this vision ends with an exposition of the role of music in the universe:

The Choirs of Angels

Spirits blessed in the power of God make known in the heavenly places by indescribable sounds their great joy in the works of wonder that God perfects in his saints . . . The song of the gladness and joy of those who tread the flesh underfoot and lift up the spirit is known, with unfailing salvation, in the dwellings of those who reject injustice and do the works of justice . . . He who strongly does the good he ardently desires shall dance in the true exultation of the joy of salvation.[3]

So music plays a significant part in linking those who value justice and express it in good works. This includes God, the angels, the Virtues as well as human beings. Our lives are to be tuned to the Virtues as seen in chapter 5 and music plays a significant part in this 'in tuneness'. Hildegard writes in the final vision of *Scivias*:

Just as the power of God extends everywhere, surrounding all things and encountering no resistance, so too the sound of human voices singing God's praise can spread everywhere, surrounding all things and encountering no resistance. It can rouse the soul lost in apathy, and soften the soul hardened by pride . . . In musical harmony you hear the victory of the virtues, as they bring people together in love and charity. In musical disharmony you hear the skills of the devil, as he tries to divide people. In musical harmony you hear the virtues enabling people to overcome their faults, and to return to God in a spirit of repentance. In musical disharmony you hear harsh sourness which lies behind the gentle blandishments of the devil.[4]

The Meaning of Music

Music is a metaphor for a symphonic view of the universe in which we are surrounded and upheld by divine Love.

> Music is the echo of the glory and beauty of heaven. And in echoing that glory and beauty, it carries human praise back to heaven.[5]

This meaning is carefully worked out in relation to the last vision in *Scivias* entitled Symphony of the Blessed. For Hildegard, this summarises all the previous visions:

> Then I saw the lucent sky in which I heard different kinds of music, marvellously embodying all the meanings I had heard before. I heard the praises of the joyous citizens of Heaven. Steadfastly persevering in the ways of Truth; and laments calling people back to those praises and joys; and the exhortations of the Virtues, spurring one another on to secure the salvation of the peoples ensnared by the Devil.[6]

Here she develops a theology of instruments. The sounds of stringed instruments call forth compassionate and remorseful tears and are associated with laments. The harp and psaltery are particularly blessed. She uses them as a metaphor for the soul's relationship to God. We need to rest in the hands of our creator like a harp in the hands of a harpist. The flute signifies the mystical union of the soul with God, the goal of all mystical activity.

Hildegard saw music as an important way of reconciling the dualism between body and soul, because it is by nature an embodied art. She saw music as a high expression of the unity between body and soul, writing:

> The words of a hymn represent the body, while the melody represents the soul. Words represent humanity, and melody represents divinity. Thus in a beautiful hymn, in which words and melody are perfectly matched, body and soul, humanity and divinity, are brought into unity.[7]

She also saw it bringing together reason and emotion, two faculties that she often perceived to be separated as she writes:

> You who know, love and adore God, with simple and pure devotion, praise him with the sound of a trumpet – that is, with the faculty of reason . . .

> And praise him with the lyre of profound emotion, and with the harp of softness and gentleness.

> And praise him with the timbrel of mortification and with the dance of exultation . . .

> And praise him with the strings of repentance, and with the organ of divine guidance.

> Praise him also with cymbals of true joy.[8]

Her high view of creation saw that God had arranged all things in consideration of everything else. She saw music as playing a very significant part in this unity:

In music you can hear the sound of burning passion in a virgin's breast. You can hear a twig coming into bud. You can hear the brightness of the spiritual light shining from heaven. You can hear the depth of thought of the prophets. You can hear the wisdom of the apostles spreading across the world. You can hear the blood pouring from the wounds of the martyrs. You can hear the innermost movements of a heart steeped in holiness. You can hear a young girl's joy at the beauty of God's earth. In music creation echoes back to its creator its joy and exultation; it offers thanks for its very existence. You can also hear in music the harmony between people who once were enemies and now are friends. Music expresses the unity of the world as God first made it, and the unity which is restored through repentance and reconciliation.[9]

Music plays a significant part in the redemptive plan of God:

Musical harmony softens hard hearts. It brings in them the moisture of reconciliation, and it invokes the Holy Spirit. When different voices sing in unity, they symbolise the simple tenderness of mutual love. When different voices blend in song, they symbolise the blending of thoughts and feelings which is the highest pleasure human beings can know. Let the sweet sound of music enter your breast, and let it speak to your heart, it will drive out all darkness, and spread spiritual light to every part of you.[10]

For Hildegard communal singing was an act of incarnation:

> Just as the body of Jesus Christ was born of the purity
> of the Virgin Mary through the operation of the Holy
> Spirit so, too, the canticle of praise, reflecting celestial
> harmony, is rooted in the church through the Holy
> Spirit. The body is the vestment of the spirit, which
> has a living voice, and so it is proper for the body, in
> harmony with the soul, to use its voice to sing praises
> to God.[11]

This is the reason for its centrality to the life of the
convent. The silencing of the music in her convent at
the end of her life would have been more significant than
the excommunication for her. It meant the intrusion of
the Devil within the walls of her convent. It is in the
letter that she wrote to the prelates of Mainz responsible
for this prohibition, that we see her theology of music
most fully developed:

> And so the holy prophets, inspired by the Spirit which
> they had received, were called for this purpose: not
> only to compose psalms and canticles (by which the
> hearts of listeners would be inflamed) but also to con-
> struct various kinds of musical instruments to enhance
> these songs of praise with melodic strains. Thereby,
> both through the form and quality of the instruments,
> as well as through the meaning of the words which
> accompany them, those who hear might be taught, as
> we said above, about inward things, since they have
> been admonished and aroused by outward things. In

such a way, these holy prophets get beyond the music of this exile and recall to mind that divine melody of praise which Adam, in company with the angels, enjoyed in God before his fall.

Men of zeal and wisdom have imitated the holy prophets and have themselves, with human skill, invented several kinds of musical instruments, so that they might be able to sing for the delight of their souls, and they accompanied their singing with instruments played with the flexing of the fingers, recalling in this way, Adam, who was formed by God's finger, which is the Holy Spirit. For, before he sinned, his voice had the sweetness of all musical harmony. Indeed, if he had remained in his original state, the weakness of mortal man would not have been able to endure the power and the resonance of his voice.

But when the Devil, man's great deceiver, learned that man had begun to sing through God's inspiration and, therefore, was being transformed to bring back the sweetness of the songs of heaven, mankind's homeland, he was so terrified at seeing his clever machinations go to ruin that he was greatly tormented. Therefore, he devotes himself continually to thinking up and working out all kinds of wicked contrivances. Thus he never ceases from confounding confession and the sweet beauty of both divine praise and spiritual hymns, eradicating wicked suggestions, impure thoughts, or various distractions from the heart of man and even from the mouth of the church itself, wherever he can, through dissension, scandal, or unjust oppression.[12]

She uses this theology (successfully) to persuade the prelates to lift their ban on her singing.

In her cosmic plan of salvation Hildegard constructed her own theology of music giving each of the five tones a meaning:

> The first tone was completed in the action of the faithful Abel through the sacrifice that he offered to God. The second when Noah built the ark at God's command; the third indeed through Moses when the law was given to him . . . But in the fourth tone the Word of the most high Father descended to the Virgin's womb and took on flesh because the same Word had mingled water with clay and thus formed man. So all creation through man cried out to him, who had made it and so on account of man carried all things in himself. At one time he created man; at another he carried him, so that all he had lost through the advice of the serpent he could draw to him. The fifth tone will be completed when all error and mockery is at an end and then all men will know and see that no one can do anything against the Lord. In this way, in the five tones sent by God, the Old and New Testaments will be fulfilled and the marvellous number of mankind completed. And after these five tones a time of light will be given to the Son of God so he will be known clearly . . . afterwards the divinity in him will be manifest, for as long as he wants.[13]

Hers was an inclusive view of music. It was central to being human:

Therefore, let everyone who understands God by faith, faithfully offer Him tireless praises, and with joyful devotion sing to Him without ceasing.[14]

It was not for a select few but intended as an essential part of the life of all human beings. Her nuns would have been selected for their religious vocation not for their musical gifts. Their musical skills would have undoubtedly increased in Hildegard's convent, but the sound of contemporary highly selective choirs may not bear any relationship to the sounds which Hildegard's nuns produced.

The Nature of Hildegard's Music

Hildegard's chants are single lines of melody using the modes (or scales) that characterise the Gregorian tradition and of varying degrees of complexity. The notation system uses symbols called neumes, which are essentially drawings of groups of notes similar to those used in the St Gall manuscript of the same period. It is the standard German Gregorian notation of the period. The notes are placed upon four or five staff lines. However, Hildegard's use of the signs and, in particular, the sign called a quilisma (written as W) is not identical with other medieval usage, so we cannot always be sure of their meaning. The neumes indicate the pitch of the notes but there is no rhythmic indication. The rhythm is dictated by the words. It is a very subtle style, reflecting the fluidity of poetic rhythms. No notational system could capture its ever-changing patterns satisfactorily. There are no performance indications or any sign of any accompanying instruments. The relationship between the various liturgical forms conforms with contemporary practice. So the hymns are the simplest pieces often using only one or two pitches for each syllable; the antiphons and responsories are the most complex using great flourishes of notes for a single syllable. These sometimes have a wide range especially the antiphon to the angels, *O vos angeli*, which ranges over two octaves. We cannot be sure at what pitch the pieces would have been sung or whether they were sung by a single voice or divided between singers with different ranges. The recordings of the groups like Sequentia achieve a delicate balance between solo and ensemble singing. The style requires each singer to enter into the dramatic nuances of the piece. These need to be blended intuitively by a group functioning without a conductor.

As with much of Hildegard's work there are significant differences from the practices of her contemporaries. The music was given as part of visions and she refused to revise them in any way. The result of this is that the music has the character of improvisation. Compared with the works of her male contemporaries, her works are free form, rhapsodic pieces, lacking the concern from symmetric construction of phrases and verses. This gives her work a flowing, unfolding quality close to a musical meditation. She draws on quite a small bank of motifs which she reworks in various forms in each individual piece. This is not unlike the techniques of traditions that are based on improvisation.

The works were thus conceived in a different way from pieces in the main European tradition, and therefore require a more cyclical way of perception, one of returning to certain ideas and motifs rather than of a steady linear progress from the beginning to the end of a score. The music is perceived as rotating around a central axis rather than a linear development of ideas. This form of construction means that her pieces do have a certain musical stability which is based not on the crafting of blocks of sound into regular strophes, but on the repetition and variation of motifs.

The structure of the words mirror this. They pile image upon image in a cumulative way. They are, therefore, not dogmatic statements of faith but discursive explorations of various themes. The songs acquire a great power based on the varied repetition of small themes, both verbal and musical. Her song texts glitter with vivid images which have been criticised in dictionaries of hymnography for their lack of structure. Hildegard took traditional subjects and reworked them in vivid and striking ways. She was not working in her native language but the associations of the images that she piles up have a dreamlike quality that would have excited the analyst, Jung. The texts have multiple meanings held together by the power of her intuition, not by her grasp of the formal strophic constructions familiar in the works of her contemporaries, Bernard of Clairvaux and Peter Abelard. Her texts cannot be read in a linear fashion because of their multi-layered multiple meanings.

This expressive style of writing is linked with a musical and verbal exuberance. There is a dramatic quality about Hildegard's work with a regular use of wider leaps and patterns based on a three-note chord that were unusual in medieval music. One of her favourite opening gestures is a leap of a fifth used as a springboard for a leap of a seventh or octave from the starting note as in the opening of O *virtus Sapientiae* (see below). She also exploits the forbidden interval of the augmented fourth in portraying the cosmic cataclysm of O *cruor sanguinis (O wound flowing with blood)*.

Medieval music uses the church modes based on ancient Greek practice. A piece usually stays within the chosen mode for the entire duration. Hildegard uses all the modes and seems to associate a particular character with each. The Dorian mode based on D has an exalted feeling, while that based on E, the Phrygian, has a sense of timelessness. She challenges prevailing practice by changing modes in the course of a piece. She ends *The Hymn to the Spirit (O ignis spiritus)* (see Chapter 10) in a different mode from the one she started in by the introduction of a B flat, challenging the tradition. Some scholars see it as changing hexachords rather than changes of modes akin to the much later device of modulation. It is out of keeping with the usage of her day. None the less in *Caritas abundat* (see Chapter 10) she changes mode to reflect the theology of the words. First it reflects the blooming of all things through the energy of Love. Finally it expresses the transformation brought about by the embrace of Caritas and the divine ruler.

The words and music are conceived as a unity and therefore are closely related. Hildegard clearly favoured and prioritised the expressive elements of music, and the subtle interrelationship between text and music in her songs illustrates this well.

In her antiphon O *virtus Sapientiae* the melody rises upwards in one of her characteristic ecstatic openings

No. 1. *O virtus Sapientiae*

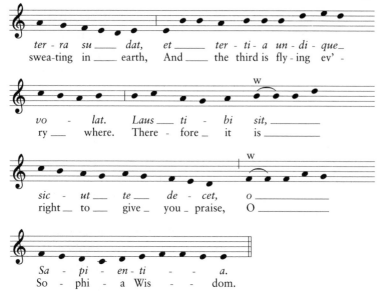

at the announcement of the power of Wisdom. In line two, concerned with circling, it circles around B. As she sings of embracing the earth in a way that brings life into being, the line sweeps down from the top E to root the life into the earth. As the first of the three wings reaches highest heaven, the line sweeps up to its highest note, while for the wing sweating in earth, it goes down nearly to its lowest note. The third flying everywhere uses the whole octave. The doxology leans downwards in a gesture of reverence.

Such dramatic writing would seem to demand a vibrant vocal style allied to her concept of *viriditas* – vibrant, greening power. There are no stylistic indications and these must be developed by each performer for her/himself. Here the text is the ultimate guide because of the unitive nature of the inspiration. It is similar to oral traditions with a measure of creativity needed on the part of the performer. Contemporary performances of Hildegard's work sometimes do not reflect such expressive writing in the chosen singing style. Having worked on her dramatic play with music I have concluded that a similar dramatic element underpins all her music. There is a lack of inhibition about the music that calls forth a similar performance style. She writes in praise of a sweet clear, ringing tone (*dulcissima, clara, sonans*) and in a letter to Elisabeth of Schoenau she compared her own voice to a trumpet resounding by the breath of God.

No accompaniment is suggested but recordings often include several accompaniments of varying degrees of complexity. These are sometimes voices, sometimes instrumental, based on the references to instruments in her writing. Gothic Voices, conducted by Christopher Page, in their measured, calm interpretation of the pieces, use instrumental drones regularly. These are also commonly used on the more ecstatic performances of Sequentia (*Canticles of Ecstasy* and *Voice of the Blood*) directed by Barbara Thornton. Here they are often performed instrumentally on the hurdy-gurdy (which is very effective if perhaps anachronistic). The Anonymous Four in their recording, *11,000 Virgins*, use a mixture of drones and unaccompanied singing. The nuns of the Abtei St Hildegard sing unaccompanied, with reverberation in the resonant acoustic of their chapel creating a kind of harmony. For her performance, the great synthesizer and cross-cultural celebrator, Sheila Chandra, uses her own style based on Indian traditions.

Other performances use the Hildegard pieces as the

basis for what are essentially new pieces. Best known of these is *Vision* which topped the pop charts in both the United Kingdom and the United States. This uses the techniques of sampling together with the complex electronically generated sounds of the pop world to create a montage that has enabled many people to bridge the gap between the twelfth and the twentieth century. Constant Mews experiments with dressing the sung texts in complex contemporary webs of sound.

Other composers have used Hildegard's music as the starting point for pieces that are distinctively their own. Lynn Plowman's *Shimmering, glimmering*, written for Adey Grummet's women's voice ensemble, *Curate's Egg*, takes *O virga ac diadema* as the basis for a complex contemporary sound canvas. My own piano piece, *Anointing the Wounds*, uses *O cruor sanguinis* as a basis for a piece following its expressive schema and with a fractal design based on its intervals. In *The Call of the Ancestors*, the antiphon *O virtus Sapientiae* intertwines Hildegard's music with improvising groups from many cultures to express the notion of Wisdom incarnating in different cultural contexts.

The Play of the Powers

The music drama *Ordo Virtutum (The Play of the Powers)* may have been written for Hildegard's novices for the celebrations at the consecration of the new buildings on the Rupertsberg. It is certainly in keeping with the way the parts for the Virtues are written, each having a short solo part and then singing in the chorus. The central character is the human soul. The heavenly powers in the form of the Virtues (who are all female) confront the lower world symbolised by the Devil. He is the only man with a significant part in the piece, making the work strikingly different from later examples of the operatic genre. There is a chorus of Patriarchs and Prophets but they only sing an opening chorus and do not appear again. At the beginning, the Virtues give the soul the pure robe of faith and she aspires to be one of them. But before she can be fully integrated with them, the Devil appears and attracts her attention. The soul struggles with her calling to heavenly things but in the end decides that it is too difficult and casts off the robe of faith. She is promised honour in the eyes of the world. The Virtues lament her loss and the apparent victory of the Devil. He replies with insults but he is unable to hurt them. They gather together. Each Virtue introduces herself with her character carefully drawn. The other Virtues affirm the singer. For example, Victory organising the Virtues for their final onslaught on the Devil reaches some of the highest notes, whereas the gentler Humility and Chastity have their parts pitched in a much lower register with less strident turns of phrase. The soul returns bruised and battered by her experience in the world. She cries out for help from the Virtues and they comfort her and clothe her again in the robe of faith. The Devil's plans have been defeated. He makes one last appeal but the soul rejects him once and for all. The Virtues are victorious and fall upon the Devil and bind him up in a dramatic scene that resembles Michael and the angels' victory in the Book of Revelation.

As a mystical play, the drama is quite statuesque, the

interest lying primarily in the way in which the allegorical themes are developed in the music. The piece is 'through-composed', which means that there are no passages that recur exactly, although the music is constructed from a number of small melodic motifs as described above. The text and melody are closely bound together and there are clear examples of word-painting as in the running group of notes when the soul sings of running from the Devil. It is difficult to grasp the dramatic quality in audio-recordings. The videotape produced by Vox Animae beautifully set in an ancient abbey is a fine introduction to it. Such performances demand a massive co-operation between scholars, performers, composers, dancers and dramatic producers to bring the works to life.

Summary

Music was central to Hildegard's concept of harmonious living. Her own music given as part of her visions, summarises all her thinking. We cannot fully understand the dramatic nature of these manifestations of the divine will that she received. She blends words and music in a unique way that represents a divine incarnation that is a source of much inspiration today.

Exercises

1. Use the mandala of the angels to meditate on the interconnectedness of the cosmos. Trace the circles of the angels with your finger and sing or hum while

you do this. Imagine your song going out into the world and connecting you with all beings who seek justice.

2. Listen to a favourite piece of music. Allow it to enter your being. Pray with it.

3. (a) Produce your own piece of meditative writing by contemplating a beautiful object and writing a stream of free association. Compare it with Hildegard's free flowing images.

(b) Now use the same technique to improvise a song.

4. Listen to one of the recordings of Hildegard's music. Allow it to enter into your soul and imagine it nourishing you. Find yourself a private place and fill it with a fragrance that you enjoy; get the lighting subdued, perhaps using candles. Find a comfortable place where you can lie with the sound source within your reach. Lie there and gently relax. Concentrate on your breathing. Hum gently on the out breath and feel the sound circle within you. Set the music playing and allow your thoughts to follow the flow of the music. Feel the sounds surrounding you, bathing you. Imagine a white light filling your being and allow the line of the music to carry it around the body.

A WOMAN FOR OUR TIME

Hymn

1. Hildegard of faith unbending,
   Father on the breath of God,
   World of substance all transcending,
   Treading paths as yet untrod,
   In discernment travelled forward,
   Penetrating Wisdom's knot.

2. Lonely woman, silence keeping
   Till the time to speak came near,
   Then the praise of God unceasing
   From your lips the world could hear;
   Justice for a whole creation
   Underpinned your message clear.

3. May discernment bring us wisdom.
   In compassion may we love.
   Deep in joy may we find laughter.
   May our trust be just enough,
   So that, dancing, we may enter,
   Shining courts in heav'n above

   June Boyce-Tillman

What is it that makes Hildegard so significant for the twenty-first century? Why has her music reached the top of both classical and popular charts? This book has examined the way she worked out her theology in her life and in her writings. It has shown that although she was the product of medieval systems of thought, she added her own unique stamp to everything that she undertook. It has shown how those ways of knowing are different from the dominant traditions of contemporary society. These include a trust in intuition, passionate and committed knowing and a holistic view of living. The substance of this chapter is that within her, our age finds a lost pole of human experience – a dimension that has been lost gradually, largely since the Enlightenment, through a concentration on scientific, objective and rational ways of knowing.

Post-Enlightenment society has concentrated on and validated only one pole of human experience. Individual freedom has been valued above community, reason above emotion, product rather than process, order above chaos, conformity rather than diversity, to name but a few of the potential polarities. Many post-Enlightenment thinkers including significant figures such as the educator Froebel and the philosopher Dewey have called for a need to explore both of these apparent polarities. And yet Western society shows no sign of relaxing its validation of one of these polarities and its marginalisation of the other. Science and mathematics now dominate education, and the arts are pushed to the margins. Capitalism deals only in products and cares nothing for process. British society has become more norm-based in the last twenty years with its establishment of fixed procedures and codes of practice so that more and more people are pushed to the margins as evidenced by increases in mental illness and the need for new prisons. Linear thinking, moving to truth by carefully planned steps, holds sway over more circular forms of creativity embracing a descent into chaos as a necessary part of the creative process. Hildegard recalls an age before the domination of this mode of thinking and opens up the possibility of new ways of understanding. As a figure from history she presents this not as a contemporary revolution, but as a recovery of a lost tradition from the past.

Connected Knowing

Our society has shown its preference for discrete forms of knowledge. In the United Kingdom the school curriculum is divided into separate subjects even in work with the youngest children. We now have a situation where after a day's outing to the farm nursery teachers have to tease out which aspects were maths, science, geography, music, technology and so on. It is, I suggest, not the way that most of us experience the world, and needs to be balanced by a way of seeing the world as interrelated and connected. The notion of separating the various areas of knowledge appeared in Europe after Hildegard. We have seen how for Hildegard the notion of justice was about right relationship and how God arranged each thing in relationship to everything else.

Contemporary musicians and healers are using Hildegard's music as a way of bringing the physical, psychological and spiritual together. To manage the long phrases of her music can cause hyperventilation, which induces a meditative state. The breath of the physical body becomes a living metaphor for the Holy

Spirit and each act of breathing becomes an act of experiencing the divine. To sing Hildegard you are stretched to your physical limits and have a sense of singing from the deepest part of your being. Normally for us the act of breathing is an unconscious one; it carries on naturally, adapting itself to our needs without conscious thought. Singing is one of the few activities where we have to take control of the flow of breath through our bodies, to be aware of it. As such it becomes our awareness of the flow of the Spirit within us.

For Hildegard, the theory of music is inextricably bound up with the cosmic order. Her work contains mathematical proportions that reflect the patterns in the cosmos. These patterns reflect the divine plan. There is a school of contemporary music criticism that would locate themselves similarly. They stress the relationship of music to human processes, an approach which opens up the possibilities of different ways of perceiving the 'meaning' of music – ways characterised by looking not only within the structure of the music itself, but also in its relationship to the world. Hildegard's notions of the place of music in a cosmic vision illustrate this. She calls us to a perception of the possibility of ascribing a greater variety of meanings to music.

Hildegard endeavoured to see the dualisms that characterised Christian theology in relationship. This parallels developments in such areas as body theology today. Her view of the close relationship of the soul and body challenges contemporary notions of perfection in bodily shape which have in a quite insidious way been bound up with theological views of perfection. Nancy Eisland has developed the notion of the disabled God,[1] and feminist literature has drawn attention to the way notions of beauty – both male and female – are constructed by society. On a recent trip to South Africa I was welcomed at worship in St Mary Magdalene's Church, Gugulethu. I was acutely aware of a different structuring of feminine beauty within Xhosa society. My Xhosa hostess told me that the Xhosa women had said of me: 'She is a European woman but she is built like an African woman.'

Our bodies are made holy by baptism which necessarily includes all shapes, sizes and conditions of human beings; indeed those of us who do not conform to the dominant notions of beauty represent a constant challenge to that culture. The baptised body is holy, not in some form hereafter, but in its present state. That is the only logical position that a theology based on incarnation can take.

All Hildegard's work had a close relationship to the context for which it was written. There is a strong tradition of folk songs associated with work. Songs are associated with such activities as spinning, weaving and rocking the baby to sleep, stone breaking and various seafaring tasks. These songs are customised and reworked for particular circumstances. They are always being made new. The speed at which a group of tired men will break up stones is different from when they are bright and enthusiastic. The speed required for a lullaby will be different depending on the mood and the tiredness of the baby. As we listen to Hildegard's music today it is impossible for us to ascribe the meanings to it that would have been ascribed to it in her convent. Shifts of context mean shifts of meaning. For Hildegard the liturgical context would have been inseparable from the music's meaning. Contemporary culture is filled with the essentially decontextualised phenomena of the compact disc and the concert and it is difficult to enter again the liturgical context of Hildegard, except perhaps for those still engaged in the regular provision of music for worship. I sometimes imagine Hildegard transported to the front of a Mercedes speeding down the M1 and the CD *Feather on the Breath of God* playing and Hildegard saying 'But I wrote it for my nuns for the feast of St Ursula.' How it had been taken out of that context would have been beyond her comprehension.

Closely allied to the notion of contextualisation is that of ephemerality. Some of Hildegard's material may well have been lost. For many in positions such as school-teachers and church musicians, pieces are produced for particular occasions and then not preserved. I wonder how many pieces are lying around in files in contemporary convents and churches from an Advent meditation this year or an Easter celebration last year that in the end will be totally lost; indeed, it may be right that they are lost because they were too related to a particular event for wider usage. This is a changing, renewing tradition, not one concerned with preservation. The notion of eternal values has featured prominently in the history of the church and theology and it is a valuable notion; but far more hidden is the notion of the importance of the changing cycle of birth, growth, decay and death. This is the other pole of knowing where God and goodness can also be identified with the constant ebb and flow and flux that characterises the natural world. This has traditionally been allied with women because of the cyclical nature of their own bodies, seen both in the short term menstrual cycle and in the longer cycle of youth, pubescence and menopause. The fixed patterns of working life established in our society with the difficulty of allowing time for the ebb and flow of health/illness, birth/death and caring for children and work/leisure/retirement is but one example of the rigid monolithic structures (sometimes justified as being eternal in their character), inflexibly demanding on human living, which is by nature in a state of flux.

The notion of producing material appropriate only for a particular purpose, after which it will be lost or decay, is analogous to the amount of art to be found in children's clothes and patchwork quilts for beds and not on the walls of art galleries. Such artwork along with the beautifully constructed domestic table is often both useful and attractive and, as such, it wears out. Women's artworks have traditionally had this quality. Their works in the area of visual art are to be found in children's clothes and soft-furnishings which are worn out or discarded, and their musical pieces in the form of recyclable lullabies which are reworked for every new child and every new sleepless night. This notion tended to decline as, after the Enlightenment, a notion of a 'masterwork' written for all time and therefore to be preserved became the centrepiece of the history of many of the arts. The preservation of works of art in some form like musical notation became of paramount importance and the centrepiece of training in the arts. This has led to a museum-based culture which tends to look to the past as its main source for aesthetic adornment for particular occasions rather than asking current artists to tailor-make for particular events works which may not be able to be moved into other contexts or indeed should not be preserved. This way of perceiving art means that we see it always as part of the total situation with which it is connected. It can lead to the use of natural venues for the display of artworks or as settings for music making.

Individualism and Community

The classical traditions of art, especially since the Enlightenment, have stressed individual ownership of works of art, and the model of the isolated artist (which owes a great deal to the myths surrounding such figures as Beethoven) has become the artistic paradigm. Other traditions have been characterised by collaborative ways of working and a desire for community. Hildegard's music was written for her community and in her iconography she emphasises the collaboration involved in the dissemination of her visionary experiences.

Although Hildegard left her distinctive mark on all that she touched, she always stresses her relation to the divine, her being part of the tradition – her striving is for authenticity within a tradition, not innovation moving away from the preceding generation. Her fundamental desire is to belong which is so different from the individualism of the modern world. This may be a reason for the obscurity of some of her writing. Like other subject groups who wanted to exist within the established order, she invented a system of 'double speak' that could be interpreted in a variety of ways. In another similar example, the oldest layer of the black spiritual tradition in the United States has a similar double meaning. Take, for example, the phrase: 'We will gather by the river', common in many spirituals, which for the Christian overlords meant baptism, but for the black slaves meant the celebration of their own African rituals. The multiple meanings associated with this type of writing need to be read in a different way from other texts. They are often deliberately difficult to decipher and can easily be misread and misunderstood.

The European myths, such as the *Odyssey* and the *Aeneid*, underpin most of the dominant narratives of Western culture, from the ancient Greeks to *Terminator Two*. There are two roles in these epics only one of which has been explored: that is the one of the heroic journey usually undertaken by the man who moves through a series of challenges (including women) which must be dealt with and then left behind. But the other is that of the faithful Penelope left at home weaving and reweaving her tapestry, keeping the home fires burning until her husband returns home. Hers is a waiting tradition which is cyclical, not linear, a hidden tradition concerned with the maintenance of order. It illustrates the role of the preservation of tradition. Hildegard shows herself, particularly in her letters, to favour the notion of *stabilitas*. These letters often counsel monastics from engaging in spiritual pilgrimages in favour of maintaining the smooth running of their own establishments. In this she reflects St Jerome's famous injunction that it is praiseworthy not to have been in Jerusalem but to have lived well in Jerusalem.

The notion of the heroic journey has not served some

men and many women well. One of the greatest casualties today is Prince Charles. We are all familiar with Princess Diana and her role as victim (which some have perhaps rather cruelly said she played almost too well), but Charles was also the victim of the linking of kingship with the heroic myth. As such, he, the gentle visionary, was sent to Gordonstoun College to undertake a toughening course of outward bound activities, probably more suited to his sister, Anne (who as princess was not a suitable recipient for this training). The gender stereotyping of the two roles of heroic journey (linear) and preserving of family life (cyclical) has done neither men nor women any favours. It is interesting to reflect whether a 'role reversal' would have served the marriage of Charles and Diana rather better.

Hildegard and the Theology of the Feminine

Hildegard's theology of the feminine was deeply rooted in the biblical Wisdom tradition. This was not a revolution but a rediscovery of the more hidden sapiential tradition which manifests periodically in the history of Western theology. The rise in feminist theology today is evidence of a renewed search for these traditions. Feminists of many religious traditions look back to a time in the past when female images were more acceptable and chart the loss of the feminine aspects of the divine, often allying this with the loss of an authentic female voice in many faith traditions. Here Hildegard offers a model that combines male and female aspects in the divine. Her regular condemnation of her age as feminine, by which she means weak, and the importance to her of her vow of chastity does not make her a natural feminist. But what she does show is how the working out of this dimension within her theology was linked with the basis of her own authority. As such she calls us to wrestle with this dimension in our own experience and to turn it into our own experiential theology.

Intuitive Knowing

The validating of the material world above the mystical world is everywhere evident in contemporary society. The approach to conclusions by means of reasoned steps is valued above the intuitive insight based on experience. This leads to the valuing of words and numbers as sources of truth. But the sense of the mystical values the non-verbal and Hildegard's theology was generated from the visual images of her visions. She used all her creative powers to the full. In *The Book of Divine Works* she wrote: 'All arts are derived from the breath that God sent into the human body.'[2]

There were few art forms that Hildegard did not explore. Her world vibrates with colour, poetry, drama, painting, music and movement which are used in combination to reveal the truth of her visionary experience of God. Related to this is her love of the symbolic meaning of clothing. Following a contemporary performance of *Ordo Virtutum* a priest in the audience described how he had been trained to regard the female body as evil (seductive and sensuous) and how in this performance the fact that the beautifully dressed female Virtues represented goodness and the black-robed priest represented evil reversed all the non-verbal stereotypes that he had learned through his training. It is interesting to speculate about Hildegard's original intention.

The validating of the sensuous is often pushed to the margins of our culture. The mundane is often drab and unadorned, while at the edges the marginalised decorate plain walls with graffiti, children draw hopscotch plans on pavements, buskers illuminate the lives of fraught underground commuters and the rising generation indulge in the multiple piercing of noses and ears. These aesthetic additions to everyday life can serve to make us rethink the aesthetic poverty of our own lives; and help us bring aesthetics into the ordinary again.

Our culture has real problems with the visionary experience – far more than that of Hildegard. Her culture at least had a religious frame into which such experiences would fit. Having rejected this, in favour of the dominant materialism, our culture at best pushes them into the realm of the eccentric, at worst to the realm of the mad. And yet I find that such experiences are still occurring if we can create situations which are perceived as safe enough to talk about them. Leading seminars on visionaries like Hildegard, Julian and Margery Kemp, I often receive accounts of contemporary visionary experiences. Their narrators have listened very carefully to the accounts of former visionaries and find in their accounts validation of their own experiences.

In an alternative liturgy group in the early 1990s I was leading a liturgy on the Virgin Mary. She found little favour with the Roman Catholic women present who refused to read St Francis's hymn to the Virgin. After this one Protestant woman said tentatively: 'I had been using the Jesus prayer but do you know what happened?' 'Mary appeared to you,' said a woman from a United Reformed Church. 'How did you know?' said the first woman. 'Because the same happened to me,' was the reply, 'But how could I talk about it in my own church?'

The origin of Hildegard's visions in her experience of suffering (see Chapter 6) may enable us to rethink the nature of the visionary experience. Certainly the life of Margery Kemp, where we have the visions clearly related to events in her life, shows the power of the vision to heal. This is something that contemporary psychiatric medicine is only just beginning to grasp. The distinguishing of the true from the false (or helpful from the unhelpful) vision is a nettle that we need to grasp. The more scientifically based wisdom of allopathic medicine needs bringing together with the more intuitive practices that are now more likely to be found in the ranks of New Age thinkers than in Christian churches.

Hildegard's use of the more intuitive arts in healing is seen clearly in the drama she created for the exorcism of Sigewize (see Chapter 7). It is not unlike some techniques used by shamans in that the sick person is asked to enter the journey with their imagination. Her use of liturgical drama bears a resemblance to rituals being created by people today for marking significant events such as divorce, and for the healing of abuse, examples of which can be found in such publications as *Human Rites*.[3] The encapsulating of the grief at Princess Diana's death in rituals involving flowers and prayers shows a remarkable reclaiming by ordinary people of the sense and the power of ritual for personal healing.

Hildegard certainly believed that the act of singing

was power. Indeed, one can liken the silencing of her singing in the last year of her life to the cutting off of Samson's hair. Her theology of music was inclusive and non-elitist. She saw music as an essential human attribute, which no human being is intended to live without. She would have to have trained and nurtured young women who had been selected because of their vocation to God and not for their musical talent. The notion of the experienced artist as primarily an enabler of others holds sway over that of the solo artist developing singular talent by means of competition with others. The saying 'those who can do and those who can't teach' shows clearly the low esteem in which those who regard the process of nurturing others as the more important role are held.

Other instances of singing as power can be found in Western history. For example, the singing schools in eighteenth-century England played an important role in the empowerment of the working class. The women at Greenham Common were at their most problematic to the patrolling guards of the American air force base when they kept up a continuous hum. In his account of Lithuanian revolution, entitled *Revolution Through Song*, Saulius Trepekunas describes how the Russian tanks were faced with the Lithuanians singing their national songs. With the cameras of the world media trained on them, the Russians felt that they could not fire and departed, leaving the country to the Lithuanians.

And yet contemporary music education has often disempowered people by using a limited map of singing. Many stories run rather like this:

Aged four, I started school and said: 'I am Jill. This is how I dress. This is how I speak. Do you like me? This is the note I sing. Do you like it? If the note had a choirboy-type sound pitched quite high, the teacher both liked it and sang it her/himself. If, however, it didn't, I was told not to sing. The process of non-acceptance had begun.

And yet everyone has the right and need to sing as much as they have to speak. At a 'Can't sing' choir run by a friend of mine, an elderly man said to me: 'Do you know, a door has been opened to me that I thought had been shut for life.' It is interesting that he was still looking for a power that he knew was his right.

Valuing the Process

For Hildegard, process was deeply embedded in the product. Having received her music directly from God in a visionary experience, she resisted revising the pieces in any way. They therefore have an improvisatory, meditative character. This characteristic has been seen in the work of other women composers like Clara Schumann and Fanny Hensel Mendelssohn. We do not have a continuous tradition of women's classical music in Europe. If we had, this more improvisatory approach to formal structures might well have been better represented. And this may well be the choice of women, not simply the result of a lack of musical education as suggested by some writers. Hildegard also resisted traditional methods of closure like returning to the starting mode. This gives the music a sense of continuing on into the silence following the piece. She is thus setting up a different model more akin to the helix where the same point is never returned to exactly. It is a model I have followed in my own pieces.[4]

She received text and tune together which means that their relationship is extremely subtle and sensitive. In this sensitive relationship of text to tune she is in the tradition of the female singer-song writers like Joni Mitchell for whom the songs represent an intensification of her own feelings and beliefs.

If the role of process in the arts is valued, then chaos as well as order will be embraced. Linear, rational thinking has pursued order and demonised chaos. Most accounts of the creative process include a measure of chaos, indeed require it as a prerequisite for creativity. The aggressive pursuit of order over and above chaos rather than the embracing of the two in an inseparable unity has straitjacketed people into obsessive ways of thinking; and the end of it politically, when driven to extremes, is fascism, both politically and personally. In Hildegard's work with her visions we see her struggling within the chaos of quite remarkable images. It is the account of a creative person prepared to enter the chaos of such a profusion of ideas and make some sense of them.

We live in a system of capitalism, interested only in products. Everywhere we see the results of this. In schools children are assessed in one-off tests, rather than by coursework. The market economy demands products, and works of art are seen as commodities to be bought and sold and sometimes seen alongside a yacht or luxury home as a status indicator. People are seen as useful only insofar as they contribute to products. When they are tired or stressed they are replaced by other people and sent into the states of illness or retirement undervalued because they are not productive. The process used to produce the products is often soul-destroying. Human beings do not respond well to such a system. A radical rethinking is needed that puts human beings and human experience rather than capital at the centre of the organisation of society.

Hildegard's stress on the importance of the process of living (in terms of the balancing of the humours, the encouraging of *viriditas*) challenges a system that is destroying humanity. It is the system that needs challenging rather than the construction of devices to enable people to fit within it. Some schools of contemporary spirituality appear to ask people to accommodate themselves to a system when it is the system itself that needs challenging. From the Brazilian archbishop, Dom Helder Camera comes the quotation:

> When I give food to the poor they call me a saint; when I ask why the poor have no food they call me communist.[5]

Hildegard's visions are related to issues of justice. They were not private devotional experiences designed simply for her own spiritual progress. This strand of justice in relation to mystical experience needs rediscovering, to avoid the privatising of spirituality that might be in danger of rocking the boat of society (including the church) if expressed more publicly.

Holistic Approaches to Healing

In several areas today there is growth in a favouring of a more holistic approach to life that stresses the relationship of music to healing. Contemporary healers are using Hildegard's music and her remedies in particular to effect the order in these elements that she desired. In founding the Hildegard Network, bringing together people interested in exploring the links between spirituality, the arts and healing, I wanted to explore such notions. Hildegard often sounds very contemporary. For example, her belief that emotions had physical effects prefigures contemporary findings that stress and negative emotions weaken the immune system. It is the integrative aspect of Hildegard's approach which makes it so popular in contemporary society.

Passionate and Committed Knowing

The notion of dispassionate charity coloured much post-Enlightenment thinking. Contemporary theorists in many areas are challenging notions of objective reasoning separated from notions of justice and morality. What is required is a bringing together of feelingfulness and rationality as evidenced by Hildegard who, in *The Book of Divine Works*, writes of human reason and the interrelated powers of *expiratio, scientia et sensus* – spirit, knowledge and feeling. For centuries Europe has debased the will, that includes human passions, joy, hate, fear and grief, in favour of wit or knowing. Hildegard's theology expressed most clearly in her poetry and music, carrying as it does a philosophy of togetherness that was her own unique version of the thought patterns of her day, offers the possibility of moving human hearts to ecological action.

Authoritative Knowing

Hildegard learned gradually how to speak with authority. The rhythm of monastic life developed an openness within her to receive the living light in greater depth. The vision when she was forty-three, in the middle of her life, was a turning point in which she claimed God's power. This has been true of other creative women who after a mid-life crisis have found an inner strength. Virginia Woolf is but one example and the playwright, Lucy Gammon, who, at thirty-nine, wrote her first play which won the Richard Burton Prize, described the discovery that she had a voice and that people wanted to hear it as being like a fairytale. It is the rediscovery of the power of the older woman – the redeeming of the crone – who is marginalised and ridiculed by our society. Mature women today also write of such experiences.

Hildegard valued her own virginity and that of her nuns very highly. This poses some problem with contemporary theological thinking affirming the sexuality of women. However, that vow of chastity gave her the necessary separateness to realise her own potential. Only such a vow freed an aristocratic woman from the attentions of men and gave her a means of escape from the endless round of childbearing. The authority she gained in the second half of her life was gained from a mixture of a trust in God and freedom from the demands of a husband and children. This is paralleled by older single women today whose choices are affected only by time and money, giving them a better chance for unfettered self-expression than their married friends.

Even the silencing of Hildegard's voice at the end of her powerful life is paralleled in many societies today. The free expression of marginalised groups of people in contemporary society in many fields (especially artistic ones) has often been prohibited, regulated or circumscribed.

Summary

Hildegard reminds us of a way of knowing that has been lost, or rather reduced to the status of a subjugated culture, struggling to survive a dominant culture which has increasing power inextricably linked with the distribution of capital. The values of advanced capitalism need balancing with these 'hidden' values with which they need to be in relationship. These concern the need for the valuing of connection, intuition, process, holistic healing, collaboration and passionate and committed knowing. Like Hildegard we need to find again our own connected, visionary, collaborative, improvisatory, integrative, committed, authoritative song.

Exercises

1. Find an object that you have created to make your home more beautiful. Use it as the basis for a meditation on the people for whom it was made and

on the love that was woven into its making. Pray for the people and for the home.

2. Examine prayerfully your own attitude to developments in feminist theology. Read a feminist theological text prayerfully allowing yourself to accept and reject aspects of it. Look back over your own life and see how you might develop some of the ideas and images in relation to your own experience.

3. Choose a quality from this list:

joy, love, freedom, peace, shalom, calm, truth, strength, wisdom, power, compassion, energy. Reflect on it for ten to fifteen minutes. Spend a further ten minutes allowing the quality to turn into a phrase or a short sentence such as:

> I am joy.
> There is strength in the universe.
> A calm lake.

Repeat the phrase to yourself until it acquires a rhythm of the musical quality of the phrase. When you can repeat it rhythmically start softly to harmonise it with your breathing. Then sing it gently on the breath on a single note. Try various pitches until you find the one that feels really comfortable and right for you.

4. Can you think of situations where you have been afraid to speak? Meditate on them and consider what steps you would need to take to speak or express yourself with authority.

CREATIVITY

Antiphon: Caritas abundat

> Strengthening love
> Is blooming in everything,
> At her most excellent in the deeps
> And the rising stars
> And the most fascinating heart of all things,
> Because she has embraced the Highest
>   Sovereign
> In peace.[1]

The notion of *viriditas* or greening power or vitality or enverduration runs through all of Hildegard's thinking. It includes the vibrancy and energy of all creation and was perhaps born out of her experience of the lush green environment of the Rhineland. In *The Book of Life's Merits* she wrote:

> Just as the waters and the abyss show the strength of God's power, so also man's soul, which pants for God, shows its strength and power in good works. Through the hidden mysteries of his secrets, God is in the strength of the soul, as from the top down to the soles of his feet.[2]

It is this energy that gives life to the universe. This is the essence of incarnation – a process that is continuing all the time in us and in creation. Hildegard viewed the universe as process. God is continually becoming incarnate in the process of renewal that is at its heart. For her the Word is not made flesh at a particular point in history but on an ongoing basis. We can participate in this by collaborating creatively. When we undertake a creative act we become 'green'. This is so not only in an artistic act but also in working ecologically, creating relationships and working for the liberation and harmony of all creation.

The legend that Christ's eyes were green coloured much medieval thinking. It is possible therefore to equate the Holy Spirit with this greening force that flows like sap through the universe and through our souls. The opening antiphon identifies it as Caritas who is close to Wisdom (see Chapter 5). Each human soul becomes the dynamic greening power within the person. The greenness is rooted in the radiance at the heart of the universe and is gradually transformed into that light.

Hildegard saw this process in the context of an over-arching divine scheme:

> In the beginning, before the Flood, the Earth had such a greening power of life, that it produced fruits without human effort. But later, human beings neither observed discipline in worldly matters, nor did they revere God properly; they wallowed in earthly lusts. Yet after the Flood . . . between the Flood and the coming of the Son of God, flowers bloomed from the fresh sap, and through every other generative power, in a new and different way. That was because the earth was saturated with dampness of water and the sun's warmth. And just as the flowers bloomed more

profusely than in the past, the knowledge of men and women grew in the Wisdom enkindled in them by the Holy Spirit until a new star appeared. And this star indicated the King of kings.[3]

The creative act is characterised by its loss of self-awareness, absolute involvement in the present, a sense of transcendence and connection with everything. Hildegard calls us to be part of that flowing creativity and realise it in our own way.

The arts are not only expressive in their function, they also have the role of reintegration within the person. At the end of an activity we are transformed, rebalanced in some way. The activities set out below are intended to be undertaken with mindfulness, prayerfully with an awareness of the spiritual nature of this process.

The rest of this chapter will be devoted to a series of exercises based on Hildegard's *Hymn to the Spirit – O ignis spiritus*. Each will have an interior and an exterior dimension – imagination and action.

Living as Process

Verse one

> O fiery Spirit, our comforter!
> Life of the life of all that is created,
> Holy are you in giving life to all.

Exercise

(a) Imagine your life as a journey into God. Review its process. Imagine the Spirit enlivening you, flowing through you, relaxing you and enabling growth.
(b) Paint a picture enjoying the process of allowing the paint to flow across the page and unconcerned about the final product, allowing it simply to happen.
(c) Think of situations in the world where it would not be possible to concentrate on the process in this way. Is there anything you could do about these?

Healing

Verse two

Strengthening Spirit, you are holy in anointing
  the seriously broken,
Holy in cleansing weeping, infected wounds.

Exercise

(a) Imagine where you hurt. Imagine the Holy Spirit flowing through the pain. What can you do practically to help the process? Do you need to go to a health practitioner of some kind?
(b) Imagine where the community around you is

hurt. Imagine the Holy Spirit flowing through it. What can you do practically to help the process of healing?

(c) Imagine where the wider society is hurt. Imagine the Holy Spirit flowing through it. What can you do practically to help the process of restoration?

(d) Devise a healing ritual using music. You need to find a composer or a style that you feel very close to. You need to have become familiar with the music and have chosen pieces which for them represent the healing you wish, noting the changes of energy in the music. Get into a relaxed position and listen to the music with healing intention. Recognise within the music the healing work of the Holy Spirit. Experience it as *viriditas* flowing through you.

It is possible to use this process in the context of a public concert. The concert needs to be chosen carefully from the composer or style that is found helpful. Then the ritual is to attend the concert with the intention of healing a particular hurt, going through the stages outlined above. End with a blessing:

May the living Spirit carry me as a feather on the breath of God;

May the creative Spirit enable me to flower in the earth of God;

May the airy Spirit uphold me as a cloud in the sky of God;

May the watery Spirit surround me as a reed
within the stream of God;

May the powerful Spirit energise me as a leopard
in the strength of God;

May the ocean Spirit hold me as a rock within the
waves of God;

May the earthy Spirit support me as a tree within
the landscape of God;

So that in Wisdom I may reflect God's glory.

Verse three

O breathing place of holiness,

O fire of love,

O sweet flavour in the breast

And infusion in the heart of beautiful perfumes
of goodness.

Exercise

(a) Make yourself a herbal tea. Enjoy its aroma and
imagine this flowing through your being. As you
drink it imagine the work of the Holy Spirit in
you.

(b) Meditate, concentrating on your breathing.
Count to ten on the in-breath and then ten on
the out-breath. Feel the flow of the Spirit entering your bloodstream in the air.

(c) Imagine someone you know with the intention
of sending them the beautiful perfumes of
goodness.

Verse four

> O most pure flowing fountain,
> In which it becomes clear
> That God has brought together the strangers
> And is seeking the lost.

Exercise

(a) Look into a reflective piece of water or into a mirror. Be aware of yourself and your present situation and be aware of God alongside you guiding you forward and seeking you. Imagine all the aspects of your being – psychological, spiritual, and physical – especially the ones you find less attractive. Imagine where they all fit together in your being. Imagine a place for the less attractive aspects remembering Hildegard's relationships between the Powers and their twisted versions (in Chapter 5).

(b) Where in your own community could you embark on bringing strangers together or can you make relationships with the marginalised?

Committed Knowing

Verse five

> O close-fitting garment of life
> And hope of gathering all members together,

And, O sword belt of truth,
Please save the blessed.

Exercise

(a) Create your own breastplate. The breastplate,
with which we are most familiar through the one
entitled *St Patrick's Breastplate*, was essentially
a spiritual shield or strengthener that each
person constructs from objects and ideas that
they find strengthening, not unlike the medicine
shields and wheels of the North American native
tradition. Some of those made by medieval
monks and nuns survive. Think of all the things
that strengthen you, e.g. moonlight, the sea,
trees, and support of friends and family.
St Patrick uses theological images like the
Trinity and images from the natural world like
thunder and fire. Put them together in a prayer.
Imagine it encircling you. Here is a hymn that
I wrote for myself:

1. Sometimes despair comes creeping
   From shades of ancient doubting,
   And tries to get the better of
   The angel in my soul,

CHORUS

That living, loving angel
That laughs within my soul

2. Then I must look around me,
   Within me and beyond me,
   For things that gently will revive
   The angel in my soul.

CHORUS

3. The morning stars at sunrise,
   The river's rapid flowing,
   The natural world – these will embrace
   The angel in my soul.

CHORUS

4. And I must trust the smiling
   Of those whose warmth surrounds me,
   The friends who clearly recognise
   The angel in my soul.

CHORUS

5. For I must go on loving
   In brightness and in shadow
   The joy that is the lifeblood of
   The angel in my soul.

June Boyce-Tillman

(b) Are you part of someone else's breastplate?
Whom do you support and shield?

Verse six

Defend those who are imprisoned by the enemy,
And dissolve the binding chains
Of those whom the divine power would save.

Exercise

(a) See what you feel passionately about. Prayer-
    fully prepare a speech you might make or an
    article you might write. Set it in a theological
    frame like Hildegard's letters (see Chapter 2).
(b) Find a suitable forum to speak about it.

Collaborative Knowing

Verse seven

O most reliable path,
That finds its way through every place;
In the most high hills,
And in the flat plains,
And in all the deep abysses,
You bring all together and unite all.

Exercise

(a) Look at the thumb as you think of all the people
    that give you strength and support you
    Look at the index finger with its pointing quality

and pray for all who have authority over you.
Look at the tallest finger and pray for all who
have power especially the media.
Look at the fourth finger which is weak and pray
for all the oppressed.
Look at the little finger and pray for all children.
Look at how the hand is connected together and
imagine all the groups you have prayed for
in connection.

(I am indebted to Retty Foster for this prayer.)

(b) Go out and work with a new group of people that
are different from you.

Connected Knowing

Verse eight

From you the clouds stream out,
The air flows,
The stones take their character,
The waters lead out their small streams
And the earth releases its freshness.

Exercise

(a) Meditate on Hildegard's words: 'For the air blowing everywhere serves all creatures.'
(b) Draw a connected picture. How can you work
towards this vision?

(c) Think about all the different areas of life.

(d) When you get dressed in the morning do it with awareness. Be aware of the different parts of your body– of how the food that you have eaten has caused your body to be as it is – how the genes in your family have collaborated with it – of how many people have co-operated to make you the way you are.

(e) Use this prayer:

Breathe deep, breathe deep,
Feel the air move from without to within;
Three weeks ago that air was leaving the coast
  of Africa;
Now it is flowing into our lungs, into our bodies,
  nourishing us, strengthening us;
Breathe deep, breathe deep.

Breathe deep, breathe deep,
Let the air go, feel it leave,
And with it the stress; name the anxieties if you
  can;
Now the air is streaming away across the earth;
Breathe deep, breathe deep.

Breathe deep, breathe deep,
Feel the movement of the life in your body;
Feel the circling of the blood, the beat of the
  heart;
Feel the digestive juices breaking down the food
  into nourishment;
Breathe deep, breathe deep.

Breathe deep, breathe deep,
That food once lived in a field far away;
Others tended it, cherished it,
Watched it grow in wind, rain and sun, cut it
 and bound it fast;
Breathe deep, breathe deep,

Breathe deep, breathe deep,
Let the beauty from outside enter our bodies,
The love of the food growers, the industry of the
 bees and the insects,
All who have nurtured the life in the flowers
 and the fruits;
Breathe deep, breathe deep.

Breathe deep . . . deep . . . deep . . .
Feel the air . . . flowing freely . . . freely . . .
 freely
In and out . . . in and out . . . the rhythm . . .
 rhythm of living
Living . . . living . . . your living . . . our living . . .
Breathe deep, breathe deep . . .
Breathe . . . breathe . . . breathe.

                              June Boyce-Tillman

(f) Go for a walk with the intention of being aware
 of the sounds around you, even the ones that you
 don't like. As you hear each sound make your
 own imitation of it. Imitate the sounds of water,
 sirens, birds, animals, machinery, traffic. Use a
 range of tone colours including breathing with
 the wind or breeze. At first you will be very aware

of the sonic environment in which you live. By musicking you will begin to become at one with it, harmonising yourself with it. Even the less pleasant sounds will improve when you can turn them into your own version.

(g) Take a box and plant some seeds in it, being aware of the feel of the earth – the temperature, the texture, the theology.

Intuitive Knowing

Verse nine

You also always lead forward the learned
Through the inspiration of happy Wisdom.
They laugh in her joy.

Exercise

(a) Meditate on a funny story of your choosing. Enjoy the laughter.

(b) Do you accept your visions? Can you enjoy them? Write out one of them, explaining it in the way Hildegard works out the meaning of hers. Can you see their relevance in your life in terms of justice seeking?

Expressivity

Verse ten

> Therefore praise to you be given,
> Who are the sound of praise itself,
> And the joy of life,
> Hope and the richest beauty,
> Giving the rewards of light.

Exercise

(a) Imagine praise or hope and then imagine an
    object that could encapsulate the feel of it.
    Delight in constructing it. How can you share it?
    Or help others to do it?
(b) Find a piece of music that you really enjoy, poss-
    ibly one with a variety of moods within it.

- Find yourself a private place and fill it with a fragrance that you enjoy; get the lighting subdued,
  perhaps use candles.
- Find a comfortable place, where you can lie with
  the sound source within your reach.

     Lie there and gently relax (perhaps using the
  end of the *Breathe deep* poem above). Concentrate
  on your breathing. Hum gently on the out-breath
  and feel the sound circle within you. Recite the
  word 'Listen' on the in-breath, lingering over the
  final 'nn' so that it becomes a hum.
- Set the music playing and allow your thoughts to

follow the flow of the music. Note the source of the sounds . . . identify the instruments playing or the natural sounds, or the type of voice . . . Delight in the sound qualities and let them hold you in their magic qualities . . . Feel held by the sounds, surrounded by them, bathed with them. Go with them. Listen deeply . . . If you have difficulty concentrating return to the word 'Listen' again.

- What do you feel? Are these images in your mind? Follow the images to where they lead. See how they merge one into the other . . . keep them moving gently forward with the music.
- If thoughts from outside the music occur, return again to the music identifying the sound sources again.
- If you get an unpleasant image let it go as the music moves forward . . . if it will not go, return to the sounds again, identifying them, letting them hold you and carry you.
- Feel the flow of the energy inside you following the changes of the music . . . let the images follow the rhythm of the expression of the music; follow the flow of the music and sense its effect on your body . . . your mind . . . your spirit . . . let it take you . . . give yourself to it.
- As it comes to end, let your mind and body come to rest. Return to the room, its perfume, its lighting, its privacy.
- Now you have explored the space of the music every time you play it you will revisit this place.

Conclusion

I have created a metric version of Hildegard's hymn. Try creating a tune for it. Start simply by chanting or singing freely and keep singing until it forms into a tune. Alternatively find a tune that you like and try singing the hymn to it:

1. Spirit of fire, you lead the way
   Through mountain and abyss,
   A path that's safe, which we can trust
   To lead us to our bliss.

2. Holy you are in giving life
   To everything we know;
   And holy too because your love
   Through weeping wounds can flow.

3. Spirit of fire, infuse our hearts
   With aromatic balm;
   Anoint our lives with healing oil;
   Preserve us from all harm.

4. Spirit of fire, you fit us well;
   We need not be afraid,
   As your firm garment gives support
   For each one's tailor-made.

5. Spirit of fire, from you air flows,
   And rivers lead their streams;
   The character of burnished stones
   Is hidden in your dreams

6. Spirit of fire, you teach the wise
   Your Wisdom to employ;
   Their earnestness you purify;
   They laugh within your joy.

7. Praise must be sung by all to you,
   Who are their melody;
   For you are life's symphonic song
   That fills eternity.

June Boyce-Tillman

Hildegard calls us to live creatively, holistically, with commitment, collaboratively, aware of our connection with the cosmos, intuitively and expressively. In doing this we incarnate God in the contemporary world. May the *viriditas* flow through us and keep our living green with Spirit.

Final Blessing

May the strengthening Spirit bear fruit in our creating;
May the anointing Spirit touch our brokenness;
May the breath of the Spirit infuse our hearts with the beautiful perfumes of goodness;
May the flowing Spirit spring up as Wisdom's fountain in our hearts;
May the enfolding Spirit become our well-fitting garment;
May the sword of the Spirit defend our vulnerability;
May the guiding Spirit lead us through the heights and the depths;
May the elemental Spirit connect us to the natural world;

May the joyful Spirit temper the solemnity of our knowing,

So that we may become a song within the Divine creation.

June Boyce-Tillman

Notes

Chapter 2 A Woman of Her Time

1. June Boyce-Tillman, *Singing the Mystery: 28 Liturgical Pieces of Hildegard of Bingen*, Hildegard Press and Association for Inclusive Language, 1994.
2. Fiona Bowie and Oliver Davies (eds.), *Hildegard of Bingen: An Anthology*, SPCK, 1990, p. 130 (hereafter *Anthology*).
3. *Anthology*, pp. 127–9.
4. *Anthology*, p. 130.
5. Quoted in Newman, Barbara, *Voice of the Living Light: Hildegard of Bingen and her World*, 1998, University of California Press, p. 99.
6. Matthew Fox (ed.), *Hildegard of Bingen's Book of Divine Works*, Bear and Co., 1987, pp. 287–8 (hereafter *Book of Divine Works*).
7. *Anthology*, pp. 134–5.
8. *Book of Divine Works*, pp. 342–4.
9. *Anthology*, pp. 104–5.

Chapter 3 Justice and Interrelationship

1. June Boyce-Tillman, *Singing the Mystery*.
2. *Book of Divine Works*, p. 90.
3. Margret Berger, *Hildegard of Bingen on Natural Philosophy and Medicine*, Boydell and Brewer, 1999, p. 24.
4. Mother Columba Hart and Jane Bishop (trans.), *Hildegard of Bingen: Scivias*, Paulist Press, 1990, p. 161 (hereafter *Scivias*).

5. *Scivias*, p. 86.
6. *Book of Divine Works*, p. 350; letter from Hildegard to Guibert of Gembloux.
7. Robert Van der Weyer, (ed.), *Hildegard in a Nutshell*, Hodder and Stoughton, 1997, p. 37.
8. *Scivias*, p. 120.
9. Adelgundis Fuehrkoetter OSB, *The Life of the Holy Hildegard of Bingen*, Liturgical Press, 1995, p. 67.
10. June Boyce-Tillman, *Singing the Mystery*.

Chapter 4 Prayer in Community

1. June Boyce-Tillman, *Singing the Mystery*.
2. Hart and Bishop, *Scivias*, p. 227–8.
3. Ingeborg Ulrich, *Hildegard of Bingen, Mystic, Healer, Companion of the Angels*, Liturgical Press, 1993, p. 13.
4. June Boyce-Tillman, *A Life Apart*, Hildegard Press, 1995, recorded on *Singing the Mystery – Hildegard Revisited*, British music label 022.
5. *Scivias*, p. 110.
6. *Scivias*, pp. 110–12.
7. Boyce-Tillman, *A Life Apart*, pp. 20–35.
8. Quoted in Fuehrkoetter, *The Life*, pp. 28–9.
9. Ulrich, *Hildegard of Bingen, Mystic, Healer, Companion of the Angels*, p. 29.
10. Gabriele Uhlein OSB, *Meditations with Hildegard of Bingen*, Bear and Co., 1983, pp. 58–60.

Chapter 5 Wisdom and the Virgin Mary

1. June Boyce-Tillman, *Singing the Mystery*.
2. *Scivias*, p. 358.
3. *Anthology*, pp. 81–2.
4. Hart and Bishop, *Scivias*, p. 141.
5. Bruce Hozeski (trans.), *Hildegard of Bingen's Book of the*

Rewards of Life, Oxford University Press, 1986, p. 127 (hereafter *Book of Rewards*).

6. Fox (ed.), *Book of Divine Works*, p. 26.
7. *Book of Divine Works*, p. 222.
8. *Book of Divine Works*, p. 226.
9. *Book of Divine Works*, p. 204.
10. *Book of Divine Works*, p. 205.
11. *Book of Divine Works*, p. 206.
12. *Book of Divine Works*, pp. 208–9.
13. *Scivias*, p. 391.
14. *Scivias*, p. 391.
15. Peter Dronke, *Women Writers of the Middle Ages*, Cambridge University Press, 1984, pp. 186–7.
16. *Scivias*, p. 428.
17. *Book of Rewards*, p. 133.
18. *Book of Rewards*, p. 134.
19. Boyce-Tillman, *Singing the Mystery*.
20. *Scivias*, p. 133.
21. *Scivias*, p. 169–70.
22. *Scivias*, p. 170.
23. *Scivias*, p. 201.
24. *Scivias*, p. 493.
25. *Scivias*, p. 508.
26. *Scivias*, p. 499.

Chapter 6 Visions

1. June Boyce-Tillman, *Singing the Mystery*.
2. Fox (ed.), *Book of Divine Works*, p. 198.
3. Hart and Bishop, *Scivias*, p. 418.
4. Quoted in *Anthology*, pp. 63–4.
5. Quoted in *Anthology*, pp. 64–5.
6. Wanda Nash, *Gifts from Hildegard*, Darton, Longman & Todd, 1997, p. xix.
7. Oliver Sacks, 'The Visions of Hildegard' in *The Man Who*

Mistook His Wife for a Hat, Picador, 1985, pp. 158–62.
8. *Scivias*, p. 90.
9. *Scivias*, p. 73.
10. *Scivias*, p. 93.
11. *Scivias*, pp. 94.
12. *Scivias*, pp. 237–8.
13. *Scivias*, p. 371.
14. *Scivias*, p. 377.
15. *Scivias*, p. 384.
16. *Book of Divine Works*, pp. 81–2.
17. *Book of Divine Works*, p. 85.
18. *Book of Divine Works*, pp. 89–92.
19. *Book of Divine Works*, pp. 102–3.
29. *Book of Divine Works*, p. 113.
21. *Book of Divine Works*, p. 122.
22. *Book of Divine Works*, pp. 125–6.
23. *Book of Divine Works*, pp. 128–9.

Chapter 7 Healing

1. June Boyce-Tillman, *Singing the Mystery*.
2. Mary Palmquist and John Kulas (eds.), *Holistic Healing*, The Liturgical Press, 1994, p. 147.
3. Fox (ed.), *Book of Divine Works*, pp. 62–3.
4. *Holistic Healing*, p. 51.
5. *Anthology*, pp. 109–11.
6. *Anthology*, pp. 139–40.
7. Florence Glaze, 'Medical Writer', in Barbara Newman (ed.), *Voice of the Living Light – Hildegard of Bingen and Her World*, University of California Press 1988, p. 136.
8. Sabina Flanagan (ed.), *The Secrets of God (Writings of Hildegard of Bingen)*, Shambala 1996, pp. 89–91.
9. *Secrets of God*, p. 116.
10. *Holistic Healing*, p. 19.
11. *Holistic Healing*, p. 39.

12. *Secrets of God*, pp. 108–9.
13. *Holistic Healing*, p. 17.
14. Bernard W. Scholtz, 'Hildegard of Bingen on the Nature of Women', *American Benedictine Review*, 31, 1980, p. 377.
15. *Holistic Healing*, p. 167.
16. *Holistic Healing*, pp. 68–9.
17. Sabina Flanagan(ed.), *The Secrets of God*, pp. 89–91.
18. *Holistic Healing*, pp. 125–6.
19. *Holistic Healing*, p. 175.
20. *Holistic Healing*, p. 99.
21. *Holistic Healing*, p. 158.
22. *Holistic Healing*, p. 41.
23. *Holistic Healing*, pp. 55–7.
24. *Holistic Healing*, p. 85.
25. *Holistic Healing*, p. 195.
26. *Secrets of God*, pp. 93–4.
27. *Secrets of God*, pp. 101–2.
28. *Secrets of God*, pp. 97–9.

Chapter 8 The Music

1. June Boyce-Tillman, *Singing the Mystery*.
2. Hart and Bishop, *Scivias*, p. 139.
3. *Scivias*, p. 143.
4. Van der Weyer, *Hildegard in a Nutshell*, p. 80.
5. *Hildegard in a Nutshell*, p. 79.
6. *Scivias*, p. 525.
7. *Hildegard in a Nutshell*, p. 79.
8. *Hildegard in a Nutshell*, p. 81.
9. *Hildegard in a Nutshell*, p. 79.
10. *Hildegard in a Nutshell*, p. 81.
11. Joseph Baird and Radd Ehrmann (trans.), *Letters of Hildegard of Bingen*, Oxford University Press, 1994, Vol. 1, p. 79.

12. *Letters of Hildegard of Bingen*, Vol. 1, p. 79.
13. From *Vitae Hildegardis*, quoted by Sabina Flanagan in 'Hildegard and the Global Possibilities of Music', *Sonus*, Vol. 11, No. 1, Fall 1990, pp. 20–2.
14. *Scivias*, p. 534.

Chapter 9 A Woman for Our Time

1. N. S. Eisland, *The Disabled God: Towards a Liberatory Theology of Disability*, Abingdon Press, 1994, p. 31.
2. Fox (ed.), *Book of Divine Works*, p. 359.
3. Hannah Ward and Jennifer Wild (eds.), *Human Rites: Worship Resources for an Age of Change*, Mowbrays, 1995.
4. June Boyce-Tillman, 'Anointing the Wounds', piano solo based on *O cruor sanguinis*, Hildegard Press, 1996; 'The Call of the Ancestors' for brass quintet, chorus and improvising groups, Hildegard Press 1997.
5. The issues are well explored in Grace M. Janzen, *Power, Gender and Christian Mysticism*, Cambridge University Press, 1995.

Chapter 10 Creativity

1. June Boyce-Tillman, *Singing the Mystery*.
2. *Book of Rewards*, No. 22, pp. 230–31.
3. *Book of Divine Works*, pp. 231–2.

BIBLIOGRAPHY

Baird, Joseph and Ehrman, Radd (translators), *Letters of Hildegard of Bingen*, Vol. I, Oxford, Oxford University Press, 1994

Baird, Joseph and Ehrman, Radd (translators), *Letters of Hildegard of Bingen*, Vol. II, Oxford, Oxford University Press, 1998

Barton, Julie S. and Mews, Constant J., *Hildegard of Bingen and Gendered Theology in Judaeo-Christian Traditions*, Monash University, Centre for Studies in Religion and Theology, 1995

Beer, Frances, *Women and Mystical Experience in the Middle Ages*, Woodbridge, Suffolk, The Boydell Press, 1992

Berger, Margret, *Hildegard of Bingen On Natural Philosophy and Medicine*, London, Boydell and Brewer, 1999

Bernard of Clairvaux, *Letters* (trans. Bruno Scott James), London, Burns and Oates, 1953

Bowie, Fiona and Davies, Oliver (eds.), *Hildegard of Bingen: An Anthology*, London, SPCK, 1990

Boyce-Tillman June B., *Singing the Mystery: 28 Liturgical Pieces of Hildegard of Bingen*, London, Hildegard Press and Association for Inclusive Language, 1994

Boyce-Tillman, June B. *Hildegard of Bingen; A Musical Hagiography*, Hildegard Monograph Issue Two, Winchester, The Hildegard Network, 1996

Boyce-Tillman, June B., *Anointing the Wounds*, Piano piece based on *O cruor sanguinis*, London, Hildegard Press, 1996

Boyce-Tillman, June B., *The Call of the Ancestors*, Piece based on themes from Hildegard for brass quintet, choir and three improvising groups, London, Hildegard Press, 1997

Carlson, Christina M., *Woman of Words, Woman of Vision: Text and Image in the Work of Hildegard of Bingen*, Hildegard monograph No. 3, Winchester, The Hildegard Network, 1995

Eisland, N. L., *The Disabled God: Toward a Liberatory Theology of Disability*, Nashville, Abingdon Press, 1994

Escot, Pozzi, 'Hildegard of Bingen: Universal Proportion' in *Sonus*, Vol. 11, no. 1 Fall 1990, pp. 33–40

Fierro, Nancy, *Hildegard of Bingen and Her Vision of the Feminine*, Audiocassette produced by Sounds True Studio, Boulder, Colorado, 1995

Flanagan, Sabina, 'Hildegard and the Global Possibilities of Music', *Sonus* 5, Vol. 11, no. 1 Fall 1990, pp. 20–2

Flanagan, Sabina, *Hildegard of Bingen (1098–1179): A Visionary Life*, London, Routledge, 1989

Fox, Matthew (ed.), *Hildegard of Bingen's Book of Divine Works, with Letters and Songs*, Santa Fe, Bear and Co., 1987

Fox, Matthew (ed.), *The Illuminations of Hildegard of Bingen*, Santa Fe, Bear and Co., 1985

Fuehrkoetter, Adelgundis OSB (trans. James McGrath), *The Life of the Holy Hildegard by the monks Gottfried and Theoderic*, Minnesota, Liturgical Press, 1995

Furlong, Monica, *Visions and Longings: Medieval Women Mystics*, London, Mowbray, 1996

Grey, Mary, *Creation, Liberation and Praxis in the Work of Hildegard of Bingen*, Hildegard Monograph One, Winchester, The Hildegard Network, 1995

Hart, Mother Columba and Bishop, Jane, *Hildegard of Bingen: Scivias*, New York, Paulist Press, 1990

Hozeski, Bruce, *Hildegard von Bingen's Mystical Visions*, Santa Fe: Bear and Co., 1986

Hozeski, Bruce W. (trans.), *Hildegard of Bingen's Book of the Rewards of Life*, Oxford, Oxford University Press, 1994

Isherwood, Lisa and Stuart, Elizabeth, *Introducing Body Theology*, Sheffield, Sheffield Academic Press, 1998

Jantzen, Grace M., *Power, Gender and Christian Mysticism*, Cambridge, Cambridge University Press, 1995

Nash, Wanda, *Gifts from Hildegard*, London, Darton, Longman and Todd, 1997

Newman, Barbara, *Sister of Wisdom: St Hildegard's Theology of the Feminine*, Aldershot, Scolar Press, 1987

Newman, Barbara, *Saint Hildegard of Bingen: Symphonia*, Ithaca, Cornell University Press, 1988

Newman Barbara (ed.) , *Voice of the Living Light – Hildegard of Bingen and Her World*, Berkeley University of California Press, 1998

Sacks, Oliver, 'The Visions of Hildegard' in *The Man Who Mistook His Wife for a Hat*, London, Picador, 1985, pp. 158–62

Uhlein, Gabriele, OSF, *Meditations with Hildegard of Bingen*, Santa Fe, Bear and Co., 1983

Ulrich, Ingeborg (trans. Linda M. Maloney), *Hildegard of Bingen, Mystic, Healer, Companion of the Angels*, Minnesota, Liturgical Press, 1993

Van der Weyer, Robert (ed.), *Hildegard in a Nutshell*, London, Hodder and Stoughton, 1997

Ward, Hannah and Wild, Jennifer (eds.), *Human Rites: Worship Resources for an Age of Change*, London, Mowbrays, 1995

DISCOGRAPHY

Gothic Voices, *Feather on the breath of God*, Hyperion CPA 66039

Vox Animae, *The Soul's Journey: Ordo Virtutum*, Etcetera, KTC 1203

Sequentia, *Symphoniae, Deutsche Harmonia Mundi*, 77020–2–RG

Benedictine nuns of the Abtei St Hildegard, O *vis aeternitatis*, Ars Musici AM 1203–2

Vision: The Music of Hildegard of Bingen, EMI Angel Records, 521–18449

Augsburg ensemble for early music, *Hildegard von Bingen and her Time*, Christophorus, CD 74584

Viriditas, *Jouissance: Hildegard and Abelard*, 086786 344 7, (1993), Spectrum

Oxford girls choir, *Mystical Songs: The Music of Hildegard of Bingen*, (1998), CCL PT 0770

Boyce-Tillman, *Singing the Mystery – Hildegard revisited*, British Music Label, BML 022

Sheila Chandra, *The Zen Kiss*, (1994), Real World RW 45